How to Use This Book

A Variety of Presentations

1. Make overhead transparencies of the lessons. Present each lesson as an oral activity with the entire class. Write answers and make corrections using an erasable marker.

   As the class becomes more familiar with *Daily Word Problems*, have students mark their answers first and then check them against correct responses marked on the transparency.

2. Reproduce the problems for individuals or partners to work on independently. If your students cannot read them independently, you may want to read the problems aloud. Check answers as a group, using an overhead transparency to model the solutions' strategies.

3. Occasionally you may want to reproduce problems as a test to see how individuals are progressing in their acquisition of skills.

Important Considerations

1. Allow students to use whatever tools they need to solve problems. Some students will choose to use manipulatives, while others will want to make drawings.

2. It is important that students share their solutions. Modeling a variety of problem-solving techniques makes students aware that there are different paths to the correct answer. Don't scrimp on the amount of time allowed for discussing how solutions were reached.

3. Teach students to follow problem-solving strategies:
   • Read the problem carefully more than one time. Think about it as you read.
   • Mark the important information in the problem.
      What question does the problem ask?
      What words will help you know how to solve the problem (*in all, left, how many more,* etc.)?
      What facts will help you answer the question? (Cross out facts that are NOT needed.)
   • Think about what you need to do to solve the problem (add, subtract).
   • Solve the problem. Does your answer make sense?
   • Check your answer.

Scope and Sequence–Grade 1

Week	1	2	3	4	5	6	7	8	9	10	11	12	13	14	15	16	17	18	19	20	21	22	23	24	25	26	27	28	29	30	31	32	33	34	35	36
Addition Facts	•	•	•	•	•	•	•	•	•	•	•	•	•	•	•	•	•	•	•	•	•	•	•	•	•	•	•	•	•	•	•	•	•	•	•	•
Subtraction Facts		•	•	•	•	•	•	•	•	•	•	•	•	•	•	•	•	•	•	•	•	•	•	•	•	•	•	•			•	•	•	•	•	•
Column Addition	•			•			•	•		•		•		•								•		•		•	•					•		•	•	
2-Digit Addition & Subtraction						•	•	•	•		•		•				•		•			•		•		•		•		•	•		•		•	
3-Digit Addition & Subtraction						•		•		•	•	•																				•				
Read & Write Numbers	•	•	•	•	•	•	•	•	•	•	•	•	•	•	•	•	•	•	•	•	•	•	•	•	•	•	•	•	•	•	•	•	•	•	•	•
Read & Write Number Words	•	•	•	•	•	•	•	•	•	•	•	•	•	•	•	•	•	•	•	•	•	•	•	•	•	•	•	•	•	•	•	•	•	•	•	•
Count by 2s, 5s, 10s				•	•	•	•	•	•	•		•	•									•		•		•		•		•		•	•			
Ordinal Numbers													•	•	•	•		•									•									
Greater/Less Than, Equal to	•				•			•				•			•					•								•						•		•
Number Relationships		•	•	•	•	•	•	•	•	•	•	•	•	•	•	•	•	•	•	•	•	•	•	•	•	•	•	•	•	•	•	•	•	•	•	•
Counting	•		•	•		•			•							•														•						
One-to-one Correspondence		•				•			•	•		•	•	•				•					•		•	•										
Patterns				•																										•						
Fractions											•		•								•		•		•				•			•	•	•		
Shapes						•																														
Time / Calendar					•		•	•		•						•			•						•			•				•		•		
Money				•															•							•						•		•		
Weight, Length, & Capacity	•	•		•							•				•		•					•			•	•				•	•		•	•	•	
Read, Interpret & Create Graphs and Charts	•	•		•				•						•	•		•								•	•					•	•		•		•
Use Tally Marks						•																			•											

©2001 by Evan-Moor Corp.

2

Daily Word Problems • EMC 3001

Daily Word Problems

Wednesday-Week 4

Name:

The guinea pig runs around and around in the exercise wheel.

The wheel turns around 5 times every minute.

How many times does the wheel turn around in 3 minutes?

Write a number sentence here.

5

_____ times

Daily Word Problems

Thursday-Week 4

Name:

Look at the guinea pig.

Tell how many of each thing.

feet _____ 4

whiskers _____ 6

ears _____ 2

eyes _____ 2

nose _____ 1

Daily Word Problems
Friday-Week 4

Name:

The guinea pigs are lined up in their cage.

Name four different patterns you see when you look at them.

1. _____

2. _____

3. _____

4. _____

Facts About Guinea Pigs

• When baby guinea pigs are born they can see well.
• Baby guinea pigs have soft, warm coats.
• Baby guinea pigs can run, too.

14

Daily Word Problems

Wednesday-Week 6

Name:

Peanut Butter had kittens:

- one was black
- two were striped, and
- two were yellow.

How many kittens did
Peanut Butter have?

Write a number sentence here.

$1+2+2=5$

_____5_____ kittens

Daily Word Problems

Thursday-Week 6

Name:

The cat has five claws on each front paw.

The cat has four claws on each back paw.

How many claws in all? $18+18=$

$5 \times 4 = 20$

One cat has ___18___ claws.

Two cats have ___36___ claws.

19

Name:

The pet store keeps a tally to show how many kittens they sell. Look at the chart.

Kittens Sold This Month

Week 1 ⦀⦀ 5

Week 2 ‖

Week 3 ‖‖

Week 4 ⦀⦀ |

How many kittens did they sell this month? _____ kittens

In which week did they sell the most kittens? Week _____

Facts About Cats

- A cat has a sandpaper-rough tongue.
- A cat uses its tongue to comb its fur.
- A cat licks its paws and cleans behind its ears.

Daily Word Problems

Monday-Week 7

Name: _____

Each mouse had two pieces of cheese.

If there were four mice, how many pieces of cheese were there?

Write a number sentence here.

2+2+2+2=8

_____8_____ pieces

Daily Word Problems

Tuesday-Week 7

Name: _____

Dave trapped one mouse every day for two weeks.

How many mice did he trap?

Write a number sentence here.

7 + 7 = 14

_____14_____ mice

Daily Word Problems

Wednesday-Week 7

Name:

Mother mouse, Father mouse, and eight little mice live in a tree.

Three of the mice moved to a new house by the haystack.

How many mice are left?

Write a number sentence here.

8+3 =5

5 _____ mice

Daily Word Problems

Thursday-Week 7

Name:

There are four mice in the cage.

How many ears are in the cage? 8

How many tails? 4

How many legs? 16

2

🐰🐰🐰🐰 = · · · · · ·
4 4 4 4

8 _____ ears

4 _____ tails

16 _____ legs

Name:

Mother mouse had ten litters in a year. 10 ✓

Each litter had five babies in it. 5 ✓

How many babies did she have in one year? 50

How many babies would Mother mouse have in two years? 100 /100

$5 \times 10 = 50$

$5 + 5 + 5 + 5 + 5$

50
50

_____ babies in one year

_____ babies in two years

Facts About Mice

• Sometimes a baby mouse wiggles out of its nest.

• The mother mouse finds it.

• She carries it in her mouth back to the nest.

Daily Word Problems

Monday-Week 8

Name:

The squirrel collected nuts.

It had three acorns, five walnuts, and two peanuts.

How many nuts did it have in all?

Write a number sentence here.

$$5+3+2=10$$

<u>10</u> nuts

Daily Word Problems

Tuesday-Week 8

Name:

A newborn squirrel weighs about the same as two quarters.

If there are four squirrel babies in the nest, how heavy are they?

4

= 1 baby squirrel

They weigh about the same as
○ 2 quarters   ○ 8 quarters
○ 4 quarters   ○ 10 quarters

Daily Word Problems
Wednesday-Week 8

Name:

Ten squirrels were sitting on a branch.

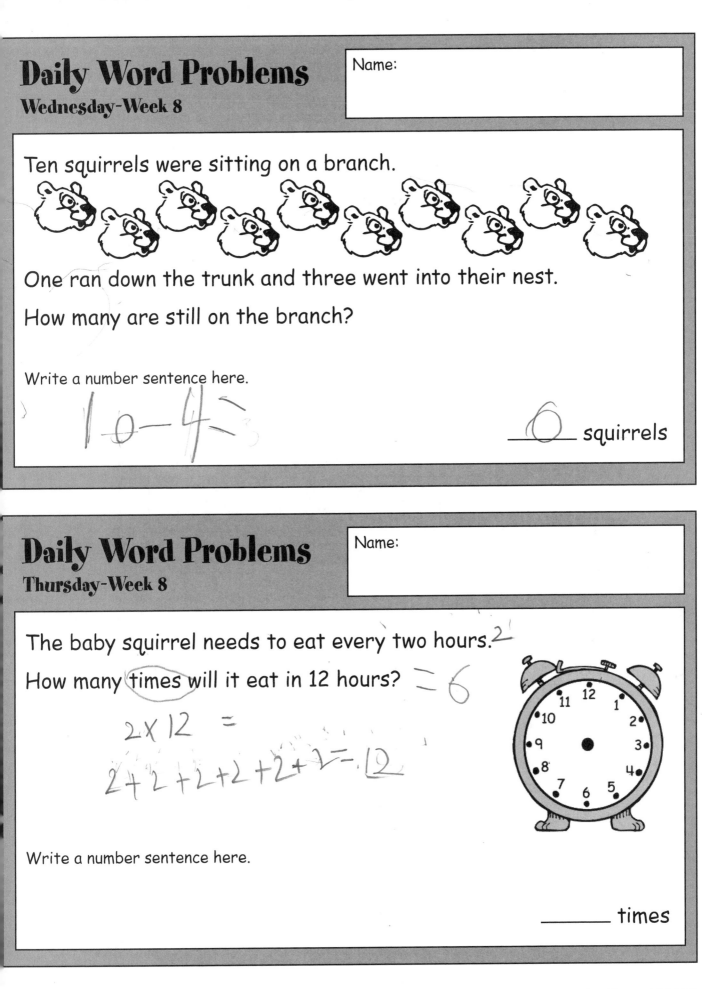

One ran down the trunk and three went into their nest.

How many are still on the branch?

Write a number sentence here.

10 - 4 =

_____6_____ squirrels

Daily Word Problems
Thursday-Week 8

Name:

The baby squirrel needs to eat every two hours. 2

How many (times) will it eat in 12 hours? = 6

2 x 12 =

2+2+2+2+2+2 = 12

Write a number sentence here.

_____ times

Daily Word Problems

Friday-Week 8

Name:

Look at the graph. Use the information to answer the questions.

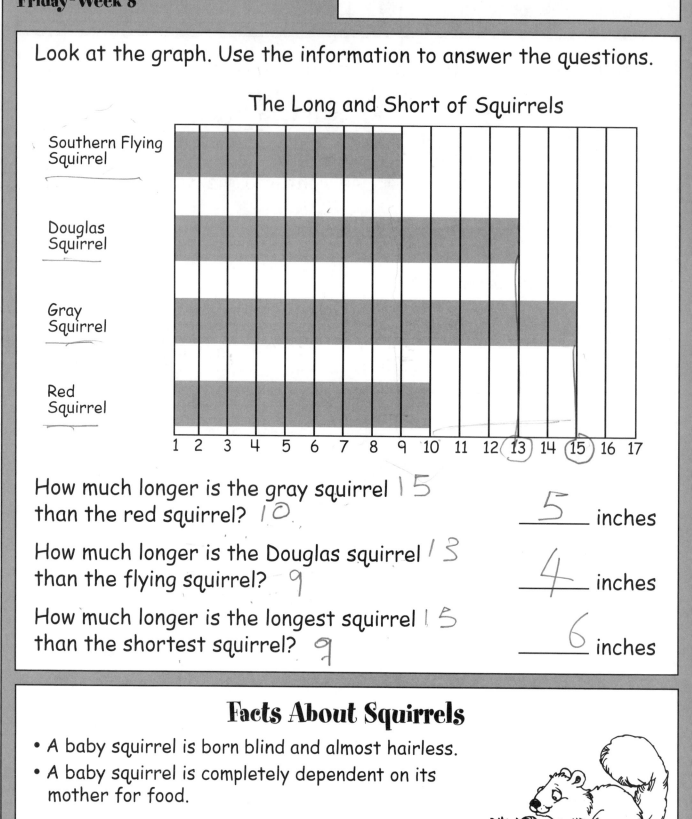

The Long and Short of Squirrels

How much longer is the gray squirrel 15
than the red squirrel? 10

_____5_____ inches

How much longer is the Douglas squirrel 13
than the flying squirrel? 9

_____4_____ inches

How much longer is the longest squirrel 15
than the shortest squirrel? 9

_____6_____ inches

Facts About Squirrels

- A baby squirrel is born blind and almost hairless.
- A baby squirrel is completely dependent on its mother for food.

Daily Word Problems

Name:

In the movie, a herd of warthogs ran across the screen.

There were six males, seven females, and ten piglets.

How many were in the herd?

_____ warthogs

Facts About Warthogs

- The warthog's piglets are born with their eyes open.
- The piglets have a coat of baby bristles.
- Their coat is striped to help them hide in the brown grass.

Daily Word Problems • EMC 3001

Daily Word Problems

Monday-Week 10

Name: _____

The mountain guides used four llamas to help them carry supplies.

Each llama can carry 100 pounds.

How many pounds of supplies did the guides take?

Write a number sentence here.

100 +100 +100 + 100 =

_4oo_ pounds

Daily Word Problems

Tuesday-Week 10

Name: _____

One guide owns eleven llamas.

If seven are being used,
how many are left?

Write a number sentence here.

11 = 7 =

___4___ llamas

Daily Word Problems

Wednesday-Week 10

Name:

Susan trained her llama to pull a cart.

She made four <u>trips</u> to the market. 4

She took four <u>bags</u> of corn each <u>time</u>. 4

How many bags did she take in all?

Write a number sentence here.

$$4 + 4 + 4 + 4 = $$

__16__ bags of corn

Daily Word Problems

Thursday-Week 10

Name:

In the pasture there are
- three white llamas, 3
- four red llamas, 4
- two brown llamas, and 2
- one spotted one. 1

How many llamas are there in all?

Write a number sentence here.

$$3 + 4 + 2 + 1 = $$

__10__ llamas

A llama eats (one) bale of hay each (week). 7

How much hay will (five) llamas need for a three-week supply? 3

5+5+5 = 21

_15_ bales of hay

Facts About Llamas

- The llama baby, called a cria, has long legs.
- A cria can walk and run soon after birth.
- A cria follows its mother as they search for a pasture.

Daily Word Problems
Monday-Week 11

Name:

Chimpanzees in the wild live about 40 years.

In zoos they live about 50 years.

How much longer do they live in zoos?

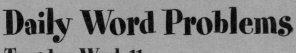

Write a number sentence here.

_____10_____ years longer

Daily Word Problems
Tuesday-Week 11

Name:
ARL

Chimpanzees live in bands.

One band has eight members and another has nine.

How many chimpanzees are in the two bands together?

Write a number sentence here.

_____17_____ together

Daily Word Problems

Name:

The chimp stuck a stick into the termite nest.

Fifteen termites ran up the stick.

If the chimp ate seven termites, how many were left?

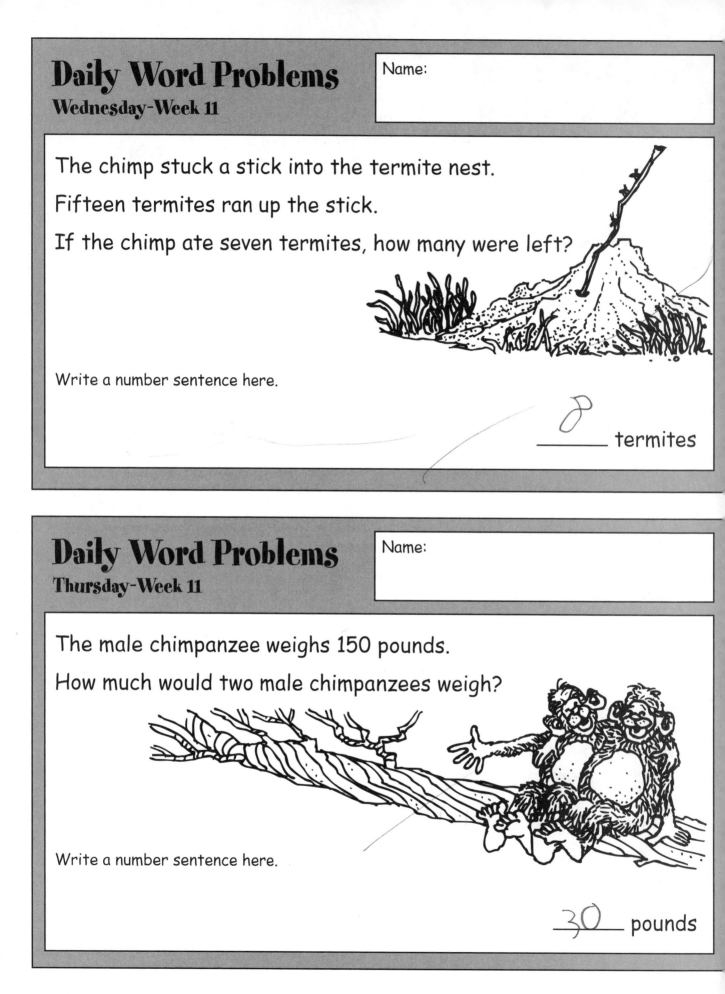

Write a number sentence here.

_____8_____ termites

Daily Word Problems

Name:

The male chimpanzee weighs 150 pounds.

How much would two male chimpanzees weigh?

Write a number sentence here.

_____30_____ pounds

Daily Word Problems

Friday-Week 11

Name:

This chimp is four feet tall.

When it puts its arms out to the sides, its reach is 1½ times as long as it is tall.

How wide is the chimp's arm span?

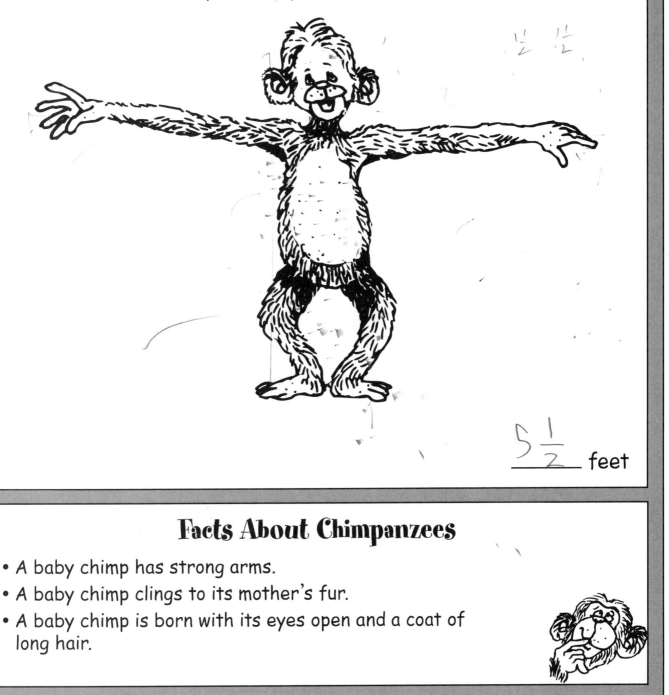

5 ½ feet

Facts About Chimpanzees

- A baby chimp has strong arms.
- A baby chimp clings to its mother's fur.
- A baby chimp is born with its eyes open and a coat of long hair.

Daily Word Problems

Monday-Week 12

Name:

There were eight polar bears on the ice floe.

Two dove into the water.

How many were left?

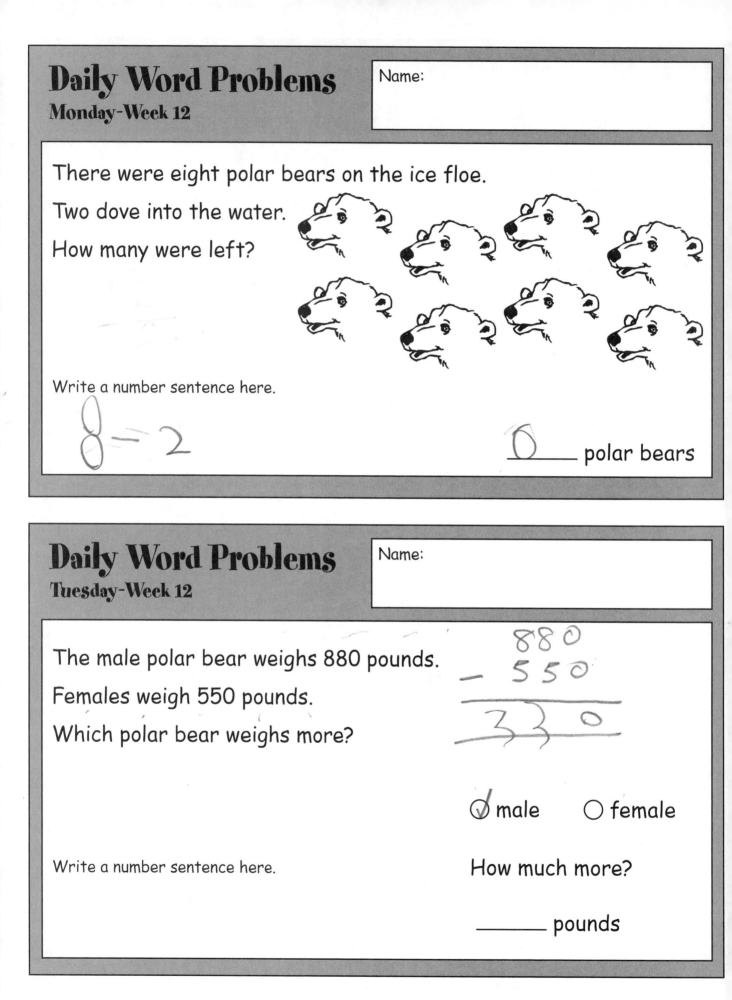

Write a number sentence here.

8 − 2

_____0_____ polar bears

Daily Word Problems

Tuesday-Week 12

Name:

The male polar bear weighs 880 pounds.

Females weigh 550 pounds.

Which polar bear weighs more?

$$\begin{array}{r} 880 \\ -\ 550 \\ \hline 330 \end{array}$$

☑ male   ○ female

Write a number sentence here.

How much more?

_____ pounds

Daily Word Problems
Wednesday-Week 12

Name:

The polar bear has five sharp, curved claws on each foot.

How many claws do two bears have?

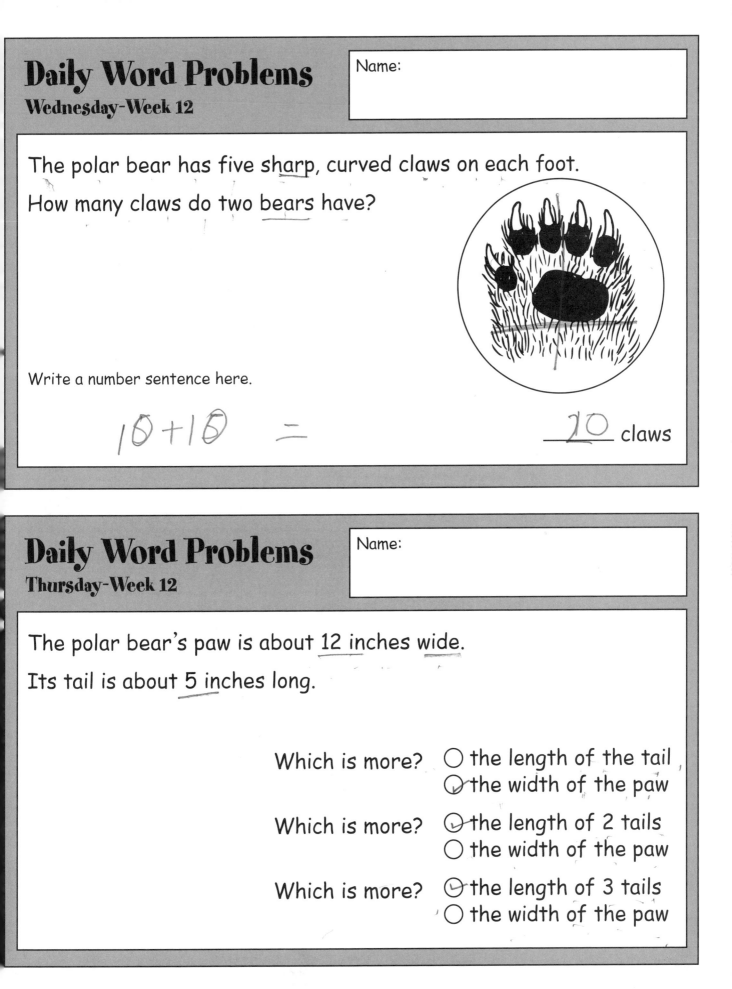

Write a number sentence here.

$$10 + 10 = $$

_____ 20 claws

Daily Word Problems
Thursday-Week 12

Name:

The polar bear's paw is about 12 inches wide.

Its tail is about 5 inches long.

Which is more?   ○ the length of the tail
○ the width of the paw

Which is more?   ○ the length of 2 tails
○ the width of the paw

Which is more?   ○ the length of 3 tails
○ the width of the paw

Daily Word Problems

Friday-Week 12

Name:

Adult polar bears have 42 teeth.

Adult humans have 32 teeth.

How many more teeth do polar bears have?

$$\begin{array}{r} 4\,2 \\ -\ 3\,2 \\ \hline 1\,0 \end{array}$$

_10_ more teeth

Facts About Polar Bears

- A polar bear cub's eyes open after thirty-three days.
- A cub's hearing is developed after sixty-eight days.
- A cub may not walk until it is nearly seven weeks old.

Daily Word Problems • EMC 3001

Daily Word Problems

Monday–Week 13

The Chinese alligator is 8 feet long.

The American alligator is 20 feet long.

How much longer is the American alligator?

Hint: Use a number line to find the answer.

Chinese

American

20 − 8

Write a number sentence here.

|||||||| ||

_21_ feet longer

Daily Word Problems

Tuesday–Week 13

The mother alligators stay by their nests.

One nest has 30 eggs and one nest has 50 eggs.

How many eggs are there in all?

30

Write a number sentence here.

_80_ eggs

Daily Word Problems
Wednesday-Week 13

Name: _____

The explorers counted <u>16</u> alligators along the bank.

<u>Six</u> of the alligators slipped into the swamp.

How many were <u>left</u> on the bank?

16 − 6 =

16
− 06
‾‾‾
10

Write a number sentence here.

_____ alligators

Daily Word Problems
Thursday-Week 13

Name: _____

The alligator's tail is $\frac{1}{2}$ of its length.

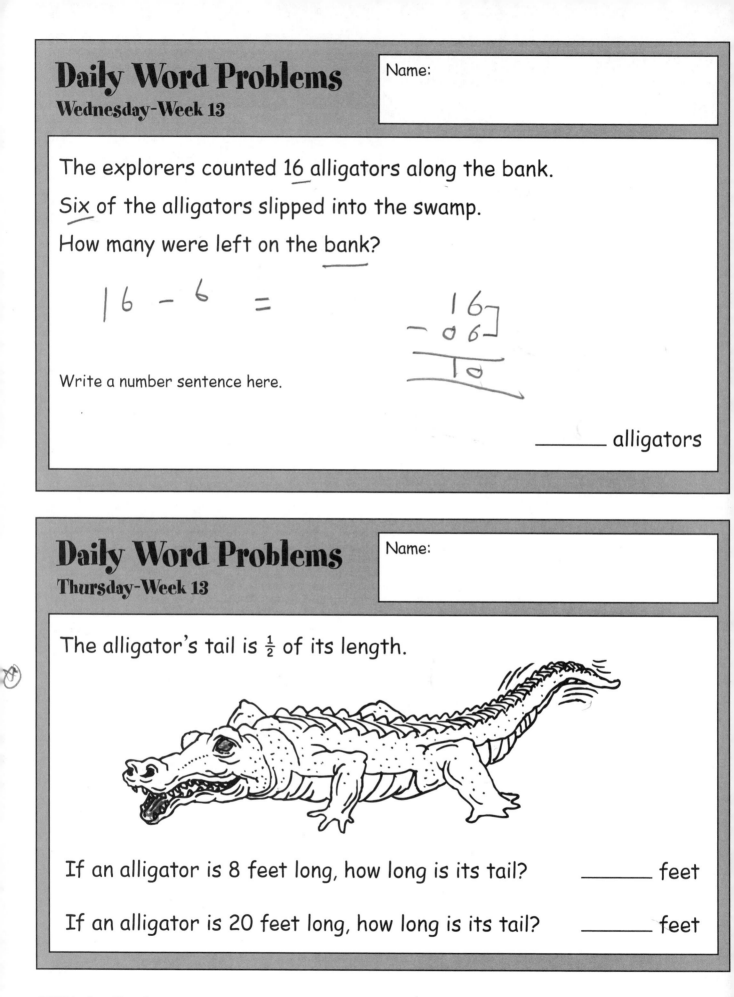

If an alligator is 8 feet long, how long is its tail?   _____ feet

If an alligator is 20 feet long, how long is its tail?   _____ feet

Name:

If Mother alligator carries three hatchlings at a time to the water, how many trips will she make to carry 30 hatchlings?

3 X 30
90

_90_ trips

Facts About Alligators

- The mother alligator carries her hatchlings to the water.
- She takes a few at a time in her mouth.
- She washes them before letting them go.

Daily Word Problems

Monday-Week 14

Name:

There are 2 koala mothers in the first tree.– 4

There is one koala mother in the second tree.– 2

Each koala mother has a baby.

How many koalas are in each tree?

Write a number sentence here.

Tree 1 has ___4___ koalas.

Tree 2 has ___2___ koalas.

How many in all? ___6___ koalas

Daily Word Problems

Tuesday-Week 14

Name:

A koala lives to be 14 years old in the wild.

How much longer will a 2-year-old koala probably live?

$$14 - 2 = 12$$

Write a number sentence here.

12

_____ years longer

42

Daily Word Problems

Wednesday-Week 14

Name:

Koalas spend about 14 hours a day sleeping.

How many hours are they awake each day?

Write a number sentence here.

_____10_____ hours

Daily Word Problems

Thursday-Week 14

Name:

The koala ate 20 eucalyptus leaves in the morning.

The koala ate 30 eucalyptus leaves in the evening.

How many leaves did it eat in all?

Write a number sentence here.

_____50_____ leaves

 Daily Word Problems • EMC 3001

Daily Word Problems

Friday-Week 14

Name: _____

Look at the graph. Answer the questions.

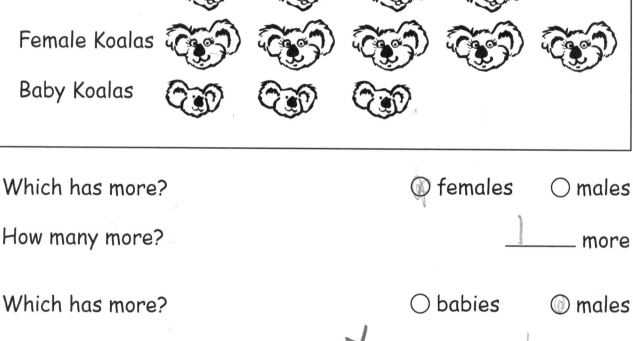

Koalas in the Game Reserve

Male Koalas

Female Koalas

Baby Koalas

Which has more?	⊗ females	○ males

How many more? ___1___ more

Which has more?	○ babies	⊗ males

How many more? ✗ ___1___ more

How many koalas are there in all? ___12___ koalas

Facts About Koalas

• Koalas live in eucalyptus trees in Australia.
• Koalas are not bears.
• Koalas are marsupials.
• A marsupial carries its babies in a pouch on its belly.

44

Daily Word Problems

Monday–Week 15

Name:

Thomas is 3 feet tall.

An African elephant is 12 feet tall.

How much taller is the elephant?

Write a number sentence here.

12 − 3 = 9

_____9_____ feet

Daily Word Problems

Tuesday–Week 15

Name:

A female African elephant weighs 7,050 pounds.

Thomas weighs 50 pounds.

How much more does the elephant weigh?

Write a number sentence here.

7050 − 50 = 7'000

7'000 _____ pounds more

Daily Word Problems

Wednesday-Week 15

Name:

One elephant herd had 10 females and 7 calves.

Another herd had 9 females and 5 calves.

How many elephants were in each herd?

Write number sentences here.

$10 + 7 = 17$

$9 + 5 = 14$

The first herd had ___17___ elephants.

The second herd had ___14___ elephants.

Daily Word Problems

Thursday-Week 15

Name:

The elephant pulls 3 gallons of water into its trunk at one time.

A gallon is 16 cups.

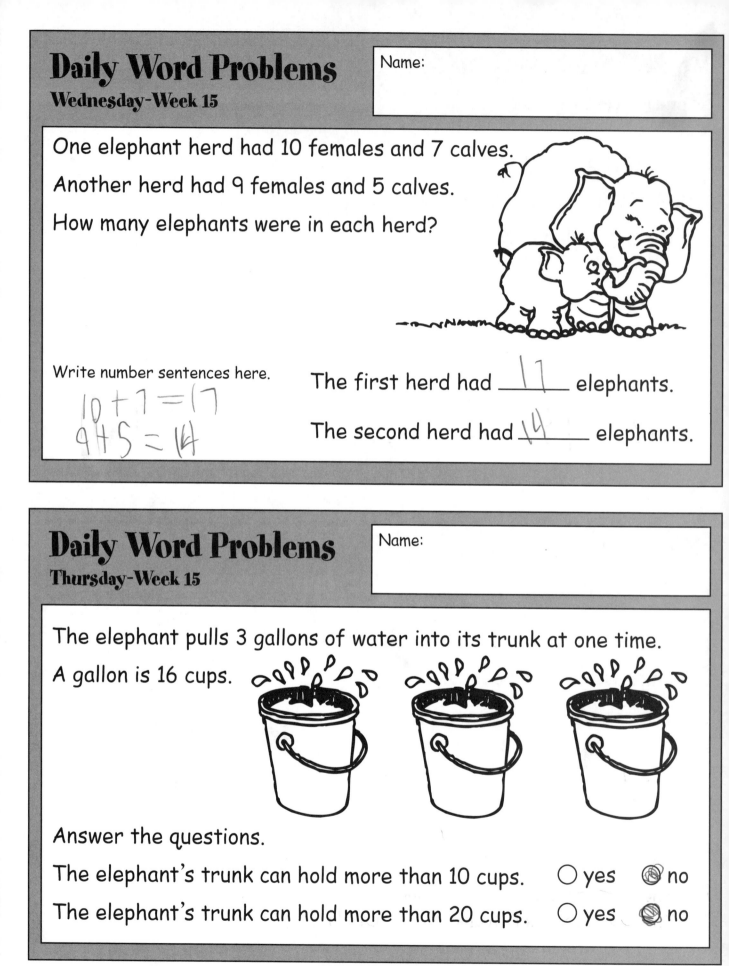

Answer the questions.

The elephant's trunk can hold more than 10 cups.   ○ yes   ◉ no

The elephant's trunk can hold more than 20 cups.   ○ yes   ◉ no

Asian elephants make a low sound that can be heard by other elephants 10 miles away.

Look at the map. Use the key to see how far it is to each elephant.

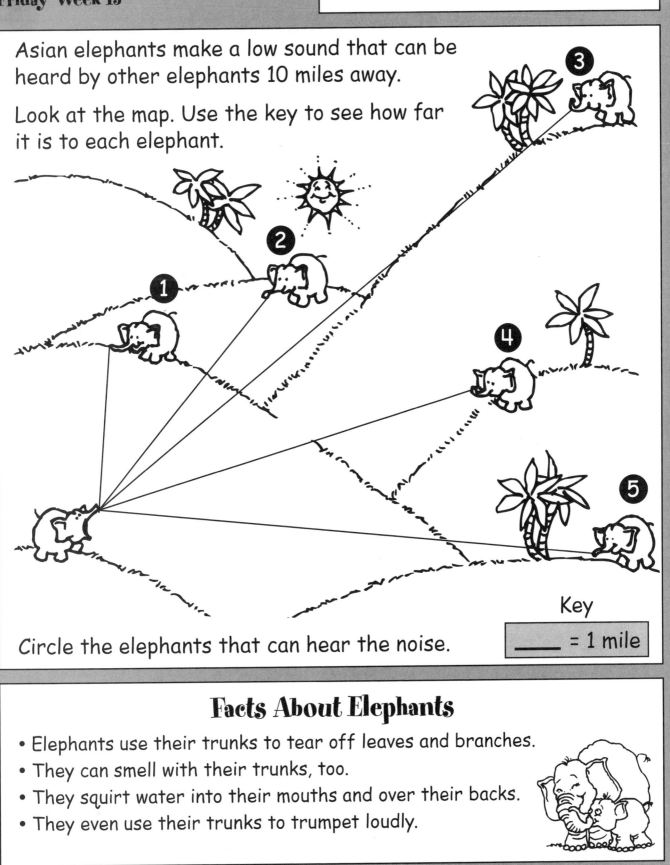

Circle the elephants that can hear the noise.

Key

_____ = 1 mile

Facts About Elephants

- Elephants use their trunks to tear off leaves and branches.
- They can smell with their trunks, too.
- They squirt water into their mouths and over their backs.
- They even use their trunks to trumpet loudly.

Daily Word Problems

Monday–Week 16

Name:

Put the camels in order by size.

7 feet

6 feet

5½ feet

7½ feet

6½ feet

Write the numbers in order.

Tallest | 7 | 6 | 5 | | | Shortest

Daily Word Problems

Tuesday–Week 16

Name:

A camel can drink 30 gallons of water in just 10 minutes.

How many gallons can a camel drink in 1 minute?

Hint: Count by tens to see how
many tens are in 30.

3

_____ gallons

Daily Word Problems

Wednesday-Week 16

Name:

A camel can go for 10 months without a drink!

| January | February | March | April | May | June | July | August | September | October | November | December |

A camel takes a drink in January. When will it need another drink?

Novermber

A camel takes a drink in March. When will it need another drink?

January

Hint: Use the list of months like a number line.

Daily Word Problems

Thursday-Week 16

Name:

Bactrian camels have two humps.

Dromedary camels have one hump.

How many humps do four bactrian camels and six dromedary camels have?

Dromedary

Bactrian

Write a number sentence here.

8 + 6 = 14

_14_ humps

Name:

When it eats, the camel eats just a few leaves from each plant so the plant is not destroyed.

Tell how many leaves will be left on each branch if the camel eats 3 leaves.

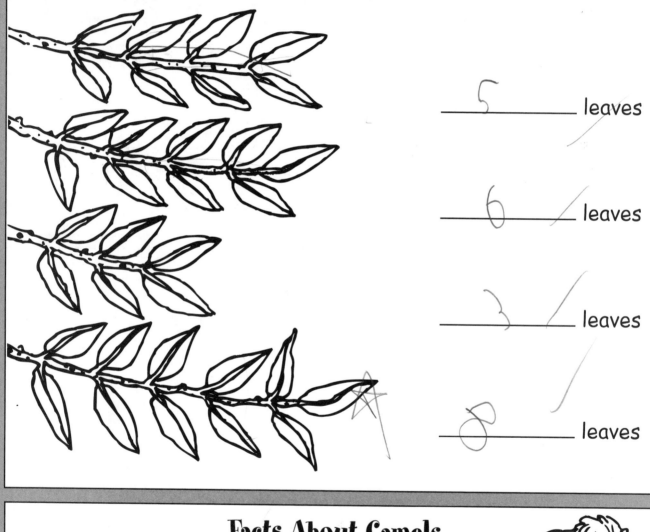

_____5_____ leaves

_____6_____ leaves

_____3_____ leaves

_____8_____ leaves

Facts About Camels

- The camel's feet are just the thing for walking in sand.
- Each foot has two big toes.
- The toes spread apart so the camel won't sink into the sand.

Daily Word Problems

Monday-Week 17

Name:

Mother fox and her five cubs were in their burrow.

Two of the cubs ran outside.

How many foxes were still in the burrow?

Write a number sentence here.

5 - 2 = 4

4 foxes

Daily Word Problems

Tuesday-Week 17

Name:

The arctic fox has a white coat.

It can jump 2 feet.

How many inches can it jump?

2 inches

Daily Word Problems
Wednesday-Week 17

Name:

4x

Mother and Father fox teach their four cubs to hunt.

Each cub catches two mice. $4 \times 2 = 8$

Mother and Father each catch three mice. 3

How many mice did the foxes catch in all?

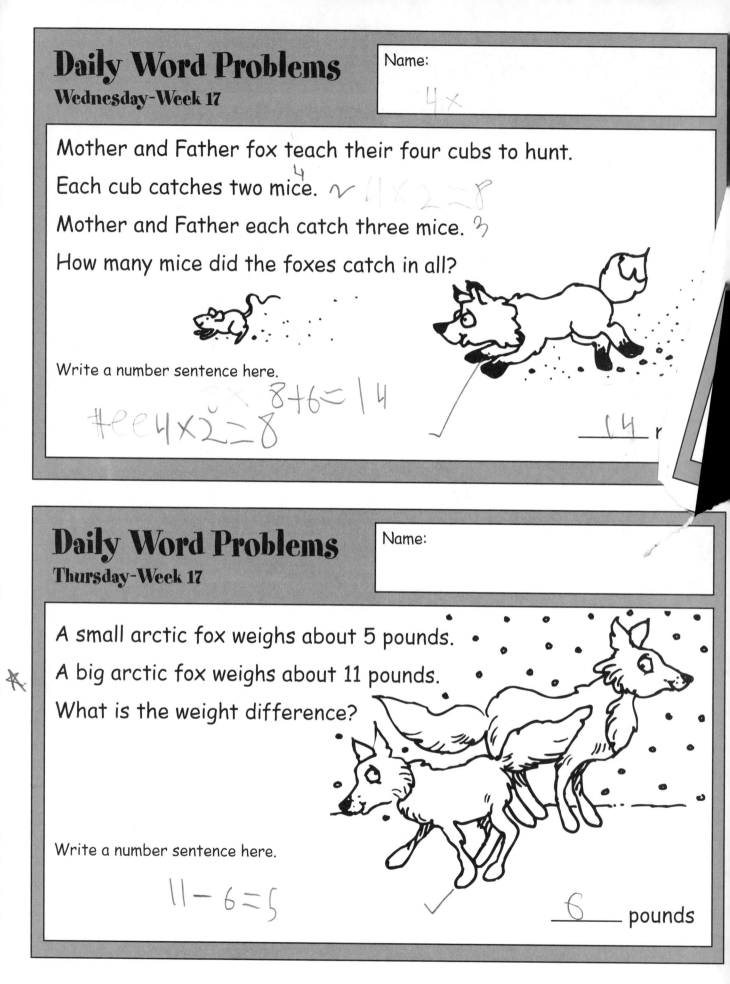

Write a number sentence here.

$8 + 6 = 14$

$\#ee 4 \times 2 = 8$

_14_ r

Daily Word Problems
Thursday-Week 17

Name:

A small arctic fox weighs about 5 pounds.

A big arctic fox weighs about 11 pounds.

What is the weight difference?

Write a number sentence here.

$11 - 6 = 5$

_6_ pounds

Daily Word Problems
Wednesday-Week 18

Name:

Four cows waited in the pasture.

Seven cows waited in the pen.

Two cows waited by the barn.

How many cows were waiting?

Write a number sentence here.

$4+2=6$ $6+7=13$ ✓

_____13_____ cows

Daily Word Problems
Thursday-Week 18

Name:

Each of Farmer Gold's cows has a calf.

If he has twenty cows, how many calves does he have? 20

How many cattle does he have in all?

Write a number sentence here.   ✓

$20+0=20$

$20+20=40$

_____20_____ calves

_____40_____ cattle

Cows' teeth are different from ours.

On the top front, cows have a tough pad of skin instead of teeth.

They have 8 incisors on the bottom front and 6 strong molars on the top and bottom of each side to grind their food.

How many teeth does a cow have?

_14_ teeth

Facts About Cows

- Cows regurgitate their food and chew cud.
- That helps them digest foods like grass.
- A cow spends a lot of time eating— up to 8 hours per day.

Daily Word Problems • EMC 3001

Daily Word Problems
Monday-Week 19

Name: _____ 6

The three-toed sloth has three toes on its front feet.

It has five toes on its back feet.

How many toes does a three-toed sloth have?

3+3 *3+3* *3+3*
5+5

10 +6

Write a number sentence here.

3 + 5 = 8

_____ 8 toes

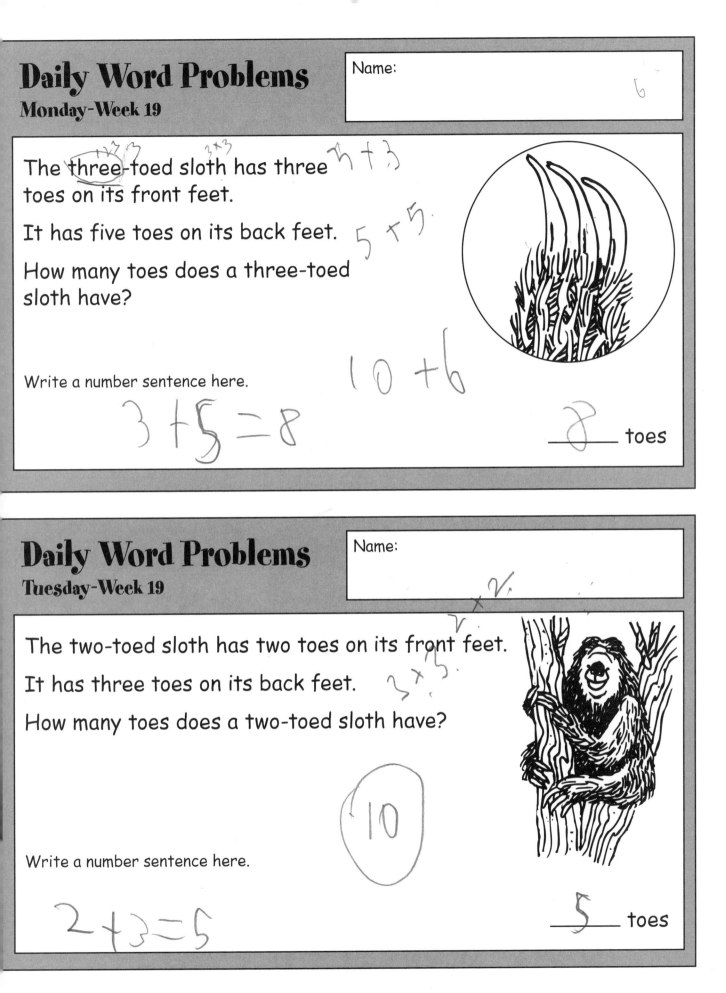

Daily Word Problems
Tuesday-Week 19

Name: _____

The two-toed sloth has two toes on its front feet.

It has three toes on its back feet.

How many toes does a two-toed sloth have?

3+3 *× 2*

(10)

Write a number sentence here.

2 + 3 = 5

_____ 5 toes

Daily Word Problems

Wednesday-Week 19

Name:

Sloths sleep about 15 hours each day.

$15 + 15 + 15 = 45$

Write a number sentence here.

$15 + 15 = 30$

How many hours does a sloth sleep in two days? __30__ hours

Three days? __45__ hours

Daily Word Problems

Thursday-Week 19

Name:

7 moths and 5 beetles live in the fur of the sloth.

How many insects make their home on the sloth?

Write a number sentence here.

$7 + 5 = 12$

__12__ insects

Daily Word Problems

Friday–Week 19

Name:

Write the names of these animals in order—the longest to the shortest.

sloth	elephant	cow
2 feet	8 feet	5 feet

alligator	mouse	
20 feet	¼ foot	

Longest

alligtor

elephant

sloth

mouse

cow

Shortest

Facts About Sloths

- Sloths spend most of their lives hanging upside down in trees.
- They live in the rainforests of South America.
- They don't clean their fur, so it grows a green scum.

Daily Word Problems • EMC 3001

Daily Word Problems

Name:

Sixteen walruses were on the ice.

Three more plopped down beside them.

How many were there in all?

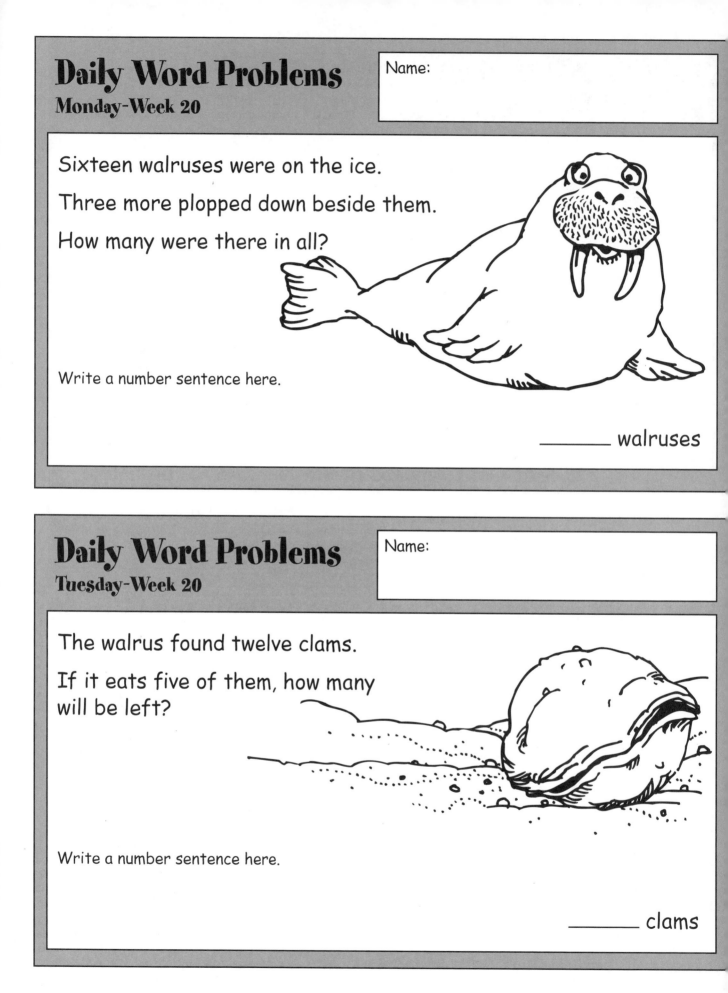

Write a number sentence here.

_____ walruses

Daily Word Problems

Name:

The walrus found twelve clams.

If it eats five of them, how many will be left?

Write a number sentence here.

_____ clams

Daily Word Problems
Wednesday-Week 20

A young walrus has 25 whiskers in a row.

It has 4 rows of whiskers.

How many whiskers does it have?

Hint: Think about 25 whiskers as a
quarter (25 cents). How many
quarters make 100 cents or $1.00?

Write a number sentence here.

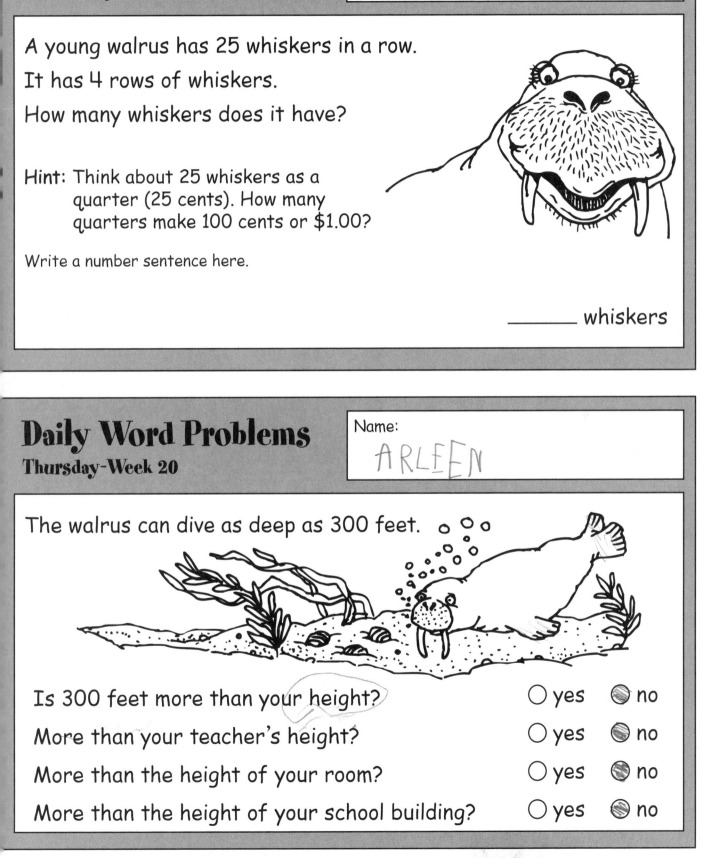

_____ whiskers

Daily Word Problems
Thursday-Week 20

The walrus can dive as deep as 300 feet.

Is 300 feet more than your height?   ○ yes   ◉ no

More than your teacher's height?   ○ yes   ◉ no

More than the height of your room?   ○ yes   ◉ no

More than the height of your school building? ○ yes   ◉ no

There is a group of 10 walruses on the beach.

How many different combinations of adults and babies could there be in the group?

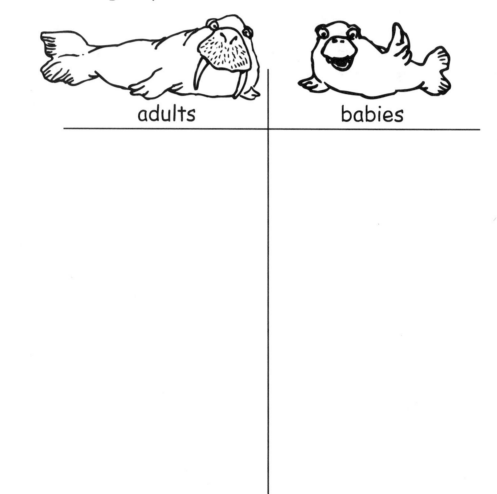

adults   babies

Facts About Walruses

- A walrus can have as many as 700 whiskers on its snout.
- A walrus uses its big tusks to climb out of the water onto ice.
- The tusks anchor it on the ocean bottom while it digs for clams.
- The walrus squirts high-power jets of water out of its mouth.
- These water jets drill into the mud and uncover clams.

Daily Word Problems

Monday-Week 21

Name:

Male sea otters weigh about 65 pounds.

Female sea otters weigh about 45 pounds.

How much more do males weigh?

Write a number sentence here.

_____ pounds more

Daily Word Problems

Tuesday-Week 21

Name:

Sea otters swim about 1½ miles per hour.

How far could an otter swim in 2 hours?

Write a number sentence here.

_____ miles

Daily Word Problems
Wednesday-Week 21

Name:

The sea otter ate five clams, two snails, and four abalones.

How many creatures did it eat?

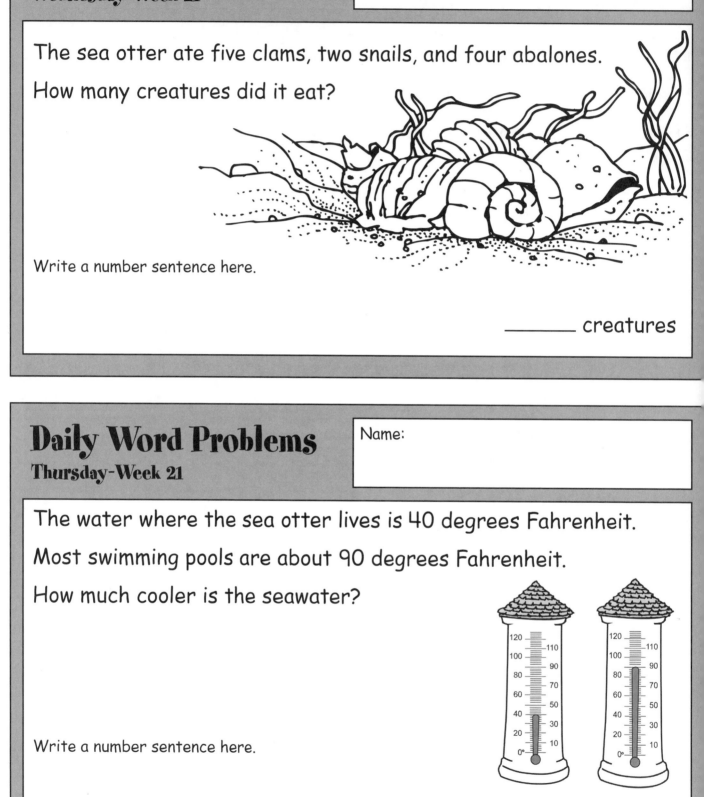

Write a number sentence here.

_____ creatures

Daily Word Problems
Thursday-Week 21

Name:

The water where the sea otter lives is 40 degrees Fahrenheit.

Most swimming pools are about 90 degrees Fahrenheit.

How much cooler is the seawater?

Write a number sentence here.

_____ degrees cooler

Sea otters must eat ¼ of their body weight each day to stay alive. If an otter weighs 40 pounds, how much food would it have to eat each day?

_____ pounds

Facts About Sea Otters

- Sea otters eat floating on their backs.
- They use their chests as tables and often balance a flat stone like a plate on their chests.
- They pound clams and crabs on the stone to open them.

Daily Word Problems • EMC 3001

Daily Word Problems

Monday-Week 22

Name:

The quills of the common porcupine are about 12 inches long.

The quills of the North American porcupine are about 6 inches long.

Which porcupine has the longer quills?

Write a number sentence here.

○ common porcupine

○ North American porcupine

How much longer? _____ inches

Daily Word Problems

Tuesday-Week 22

Name:

The porcupine is a rodent.

It has a pair of long, sharp front teeth for gnawing.

How many gnawing teeth do four porcupines have?

Write a number sentence here.

_____ gnawing teeth

Daily Word Problems

Wednesday-Week 22

Name:

The porcupine ate
- two dandelion leaves,
- four clover leaves,
- two rose leaves, and
- six leaves from a thorn apple.

How many leaves did it eat in all?

Write a number sentence here.

leaves

Daily Word Problems

Thursday-Week 22

Name:

The porcupine is Canada's second-largest rodent.

A male porcupine weighs about 6 kg.

A male beaver weighs about 16 kg.

How much more does the beaver weigh?

Write a number sentence here.

kg more

Daily Word Problems

Friday-Week 22

Name:

The porcupine has about 30,000 quills.

If a porcupine lost 1,000 quills, how many would it have?

_____ quills

Facts About Porcupines

- Porcupine babies are born with bristles.
- The bristles harden into sharp quills within a few hours.
- When in danger, a porcupine will rattle its quills and grunt.
- If this bluffing doesn't work, it backs into its enemy, quills first.
- Porcupines grow back the quills they have lost.

Daily Word Problems

Name:

Tigers are good hunters, but not all tiger attacks are successful.

A tiger is successful once in every 10 tries.

How many times will the tiger be successful in 40 tries?

Write a number sentence here.

_____ times

Daily Word Problems

Name:

In the wild, tigers live about 15 years.

Tigers in zoos live about 18 years.

Where do tigers live longer?

Write a number sentence here.

○ in the wild   ○ in a zoo

How much longer? _____ years

Daily Word Problems
Wednesday-Week 23

Name:

A tiger's tail is ½ as long as its body.

If a tail is 3 feet long, how long is the tiger's body?

Write a number sentence here.

_____ feet

Daily Word Problems
Thursday-Week 23

Name:

The Bengal tiger is 10 feet long.

The Siberian tiger is 7 feet long.

The Sumatran tiger is 5 feet long.

Write the tigers' names in order with the smallest first.

_____

_____

_____

Tell how much longer each tiger is than the one before.

_____ feet longer

_____ feet longer

In 1993 there were fewer than 6,000 tigers in the wild. Look at the graph. Answer the questions.

Tigers in the Wild

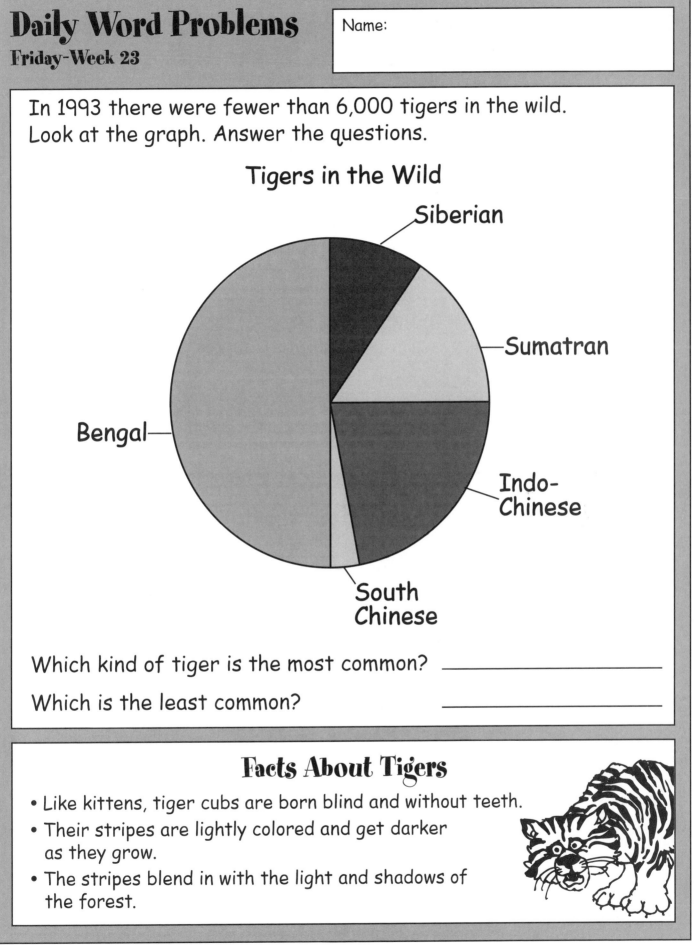

Which kind of tiger is the most common? _____

Which is the least common? _____

Facts About Tigers

- Like kittens, tiger cubs are born blind and without teeth.
- Their stripes are lightly colored and get darker as they grow.
- The stripes blend in with the light and shadows of the forest.

Daily Word Problems

Monday-Week 24

Name:

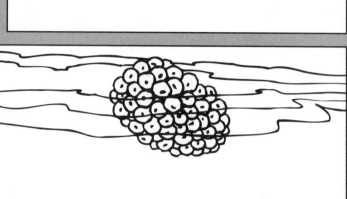

Mother bullfrog laid 24,000 small eggs in the water.

If all the eggs hatch, how many tadpoles will there be?

If all the tadpoles become frogs, how many frogs will there be?

_____ tadpoles

_____ frogs

Daily Word Problems

Tuesday-Week 24

Name:

A bullfrog can leap 6 feet.

How far will it go with four leaps?

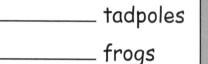

Write a number sentence here.

_____ feet

Daily Word Problems
Monday-Week 25

Name:

It takes the lowland gorilla two days to travel one mile.

How long would it take to travel eight miles?

Write a number sentence here.

_____ days

Daily Word Problems
Tuesday-Week 25

Name:

Young gorillas climb trees to find fruit and to play.

Two gorillas are in a tree.

Three more join them.

Each gorilla picks two pieces of fruit.

How much fruit did the gorillas pick in all?

Write a number sentence here.

_____ pieces of fruit

Daily Word Problems

Wednesday-Week 25

Name:

A male gorilla weighs 400 pounds.

A female gorilla weighs 200 pounds.

Compare the two weights.

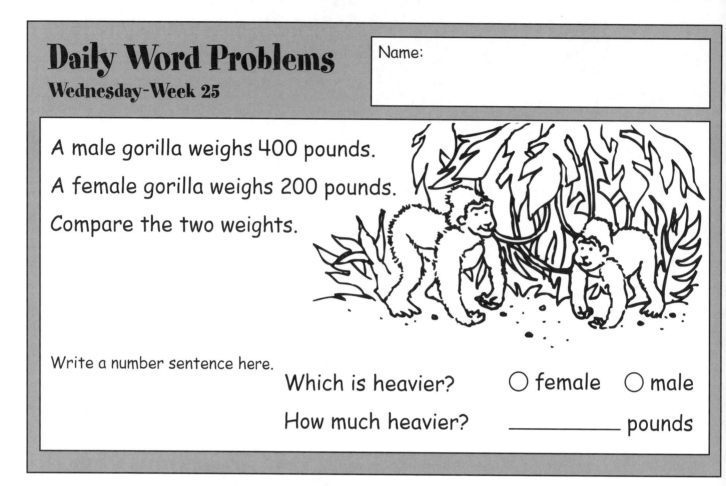

Write a number sentence here.

Which is heavier?　　　○ female　　○ male

How much heavier?　　_____ pounds

Daily Word Problems

Thursday-Week 25

Name:

The gorilla likes to eat termites and ants.

If it eats 25 termites and 20 ants,
how many insects has it eaten?

Write a number sentence here.

_____ insects

Daily Word Problems
Friday-Week 25

Name:

The gorilla spends its time eating, resting, and traveling.

Tell how long it spends doing each thing in 12 hours.

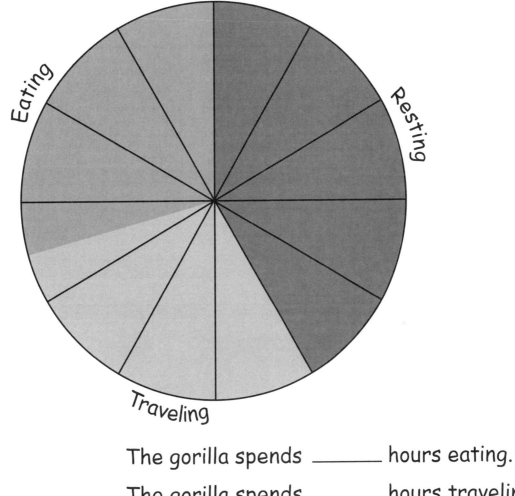

The gorilla spends _____ hours eating.

The gorilla spends _____ hours traveling.

The gorilla spends _____ hours resting.

Facts About Gorillas

- The male gorilla is the biggest primate.
- It can weigh as much as 450 pounds.
- It is a gentle, peaceful creature.
- It feeds mainly on leaves, buds, berries, and bark.

Daily Word Problems • EMC 3001

Daily Word Problems

Name: _____

The largest gecko is 14 inches long.

Some geckos are only half that long.

How long are they?

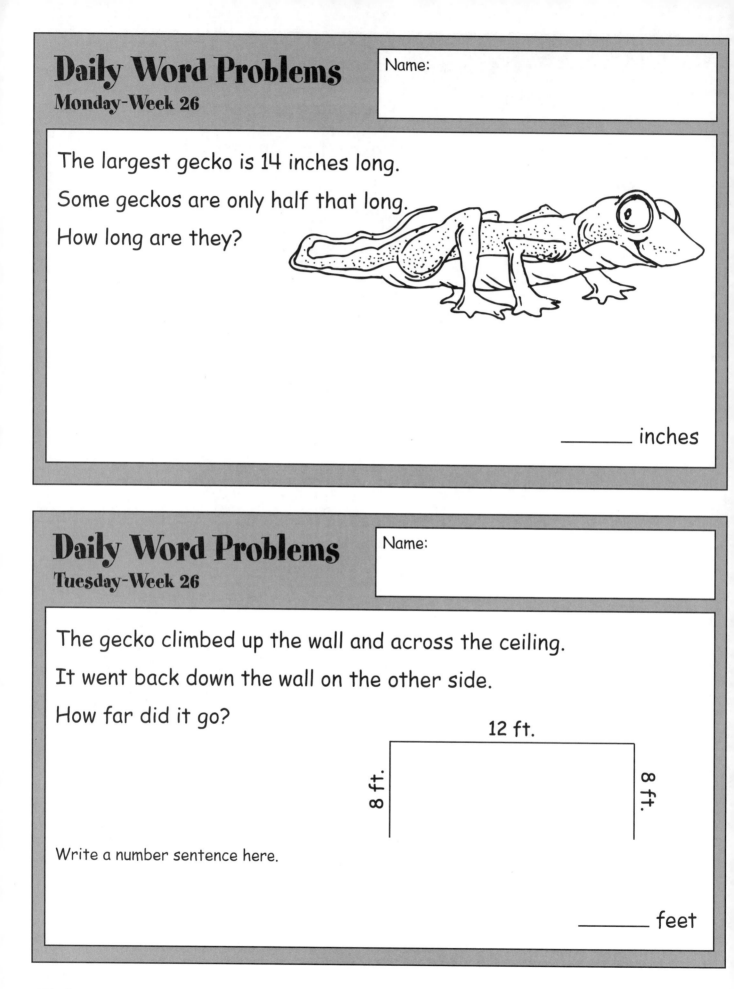

_____ inches

Daily Word Problems

Name: _____

The gecko climbed up the wall and across the ceiling.

It went back down the wall on the other side.

How far did it go?

12 ft.

8 ft.   8 ft.

Write a number sentence here.

_____ feet

Daily Word Problems

Name:

There are seven pictures on the wall.

When the lights are turned on, geckos hide behind the pictures.

There are two geckos behind each picture.

How many geckos are in the room?

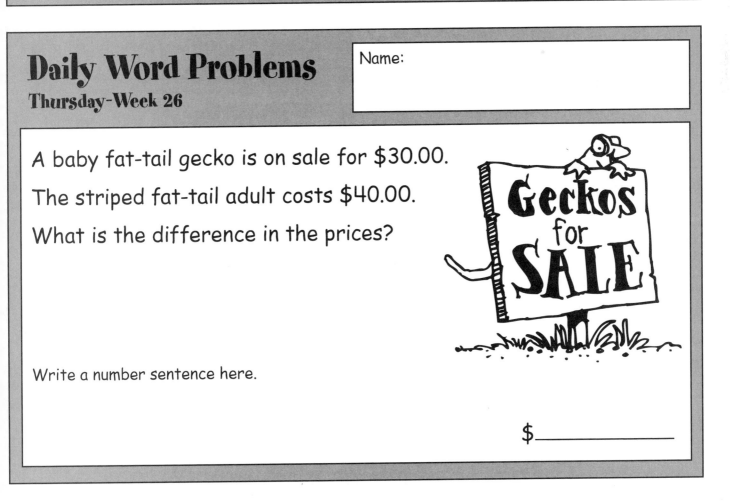

Write a number sentence here.

_____ geckos

Daily Word Problems

Name:

A baby fat-tail gecko is on sale for $30.00.

The striped fat-tail adult costs $40.00.

What is the difference in the prices?

Write a number sentence here.

$_____

Daily Word Problems

Name: _____

The visitors counted the geckos they saw in each room.

Look at the tally sheet below and then answer the questions.

Bedroom	卌 卌
Living Room	卌 卌 I
Kitchen	卌 II
Family Room	卌 卌

Which room had the most lizards? _____

Which room had the fewest lizards? _____

Which two rooms added together had
20 lizards? _____

Facts About Geckos

• A gecko is a kind of lizard.
• They are common in houses in Asia.
• A gecko has a long tongue.
• A gecko will carefully clean its face and eyeballs by licking itself.

Daily Word Problems

Monday-Week 27

Name:

The fence is 12 feet tall.

The giraffe is 16 feet tall.

How much taller is the giraffe?

Write a number sentence here.

_____ feet taller

Daily Word Problems

Tuesday-Week 27

Name:

A newborn giraffe is 6 feet tall.

If the father giraffe is 3 times as tall, how tall is the father?

Write a number sentence here.

_____ feet

Daily Word Problems
Wednesday-Week 27

Name:

A male giraffe weighs about 3,000 pounds.

An automobile weighs 2,000 pounds.

How much more does the giraffe weigh?

Write a number sentence here.

_____ pounds more

Daily Word Problems
Thursday-Week 27

Name:

There are 100 giraffes traveling in a herd.

If 20 of the giraffes stop to drink, how many are left?

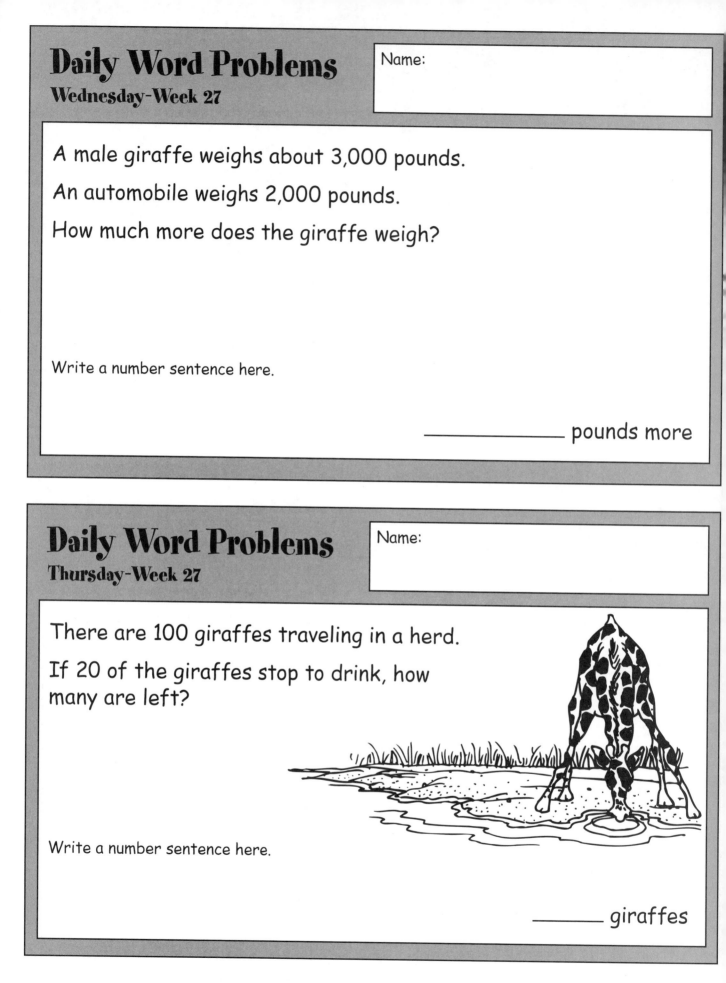

Write a number sentence here.

_____ giraffes

Daily Word Problems

Name:

Choose the best answer.

Which giraffe has horns, straight eyelashes, spots, and mane and eyes of the same color?

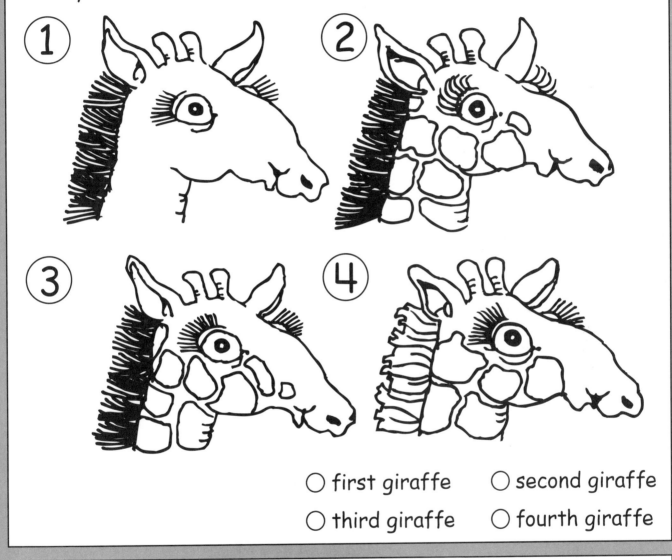

○ first giraffe ○ second giraffe
○ third giraffe ○ fourth giraffe

Facts About Giraffes

- A giraffe's tongue is 18 inches long.
- The giraffe uses it to strip leaves from thorny acacia trees.
- The giraffe prefers the new leaves and buds near the tops of trees.

Daily Word Problems

Monday-Week 28

Name:

One echidna can eat 200 grams of ants in 10 minutes.

How many grams of ants could it eat in 20 minutes?

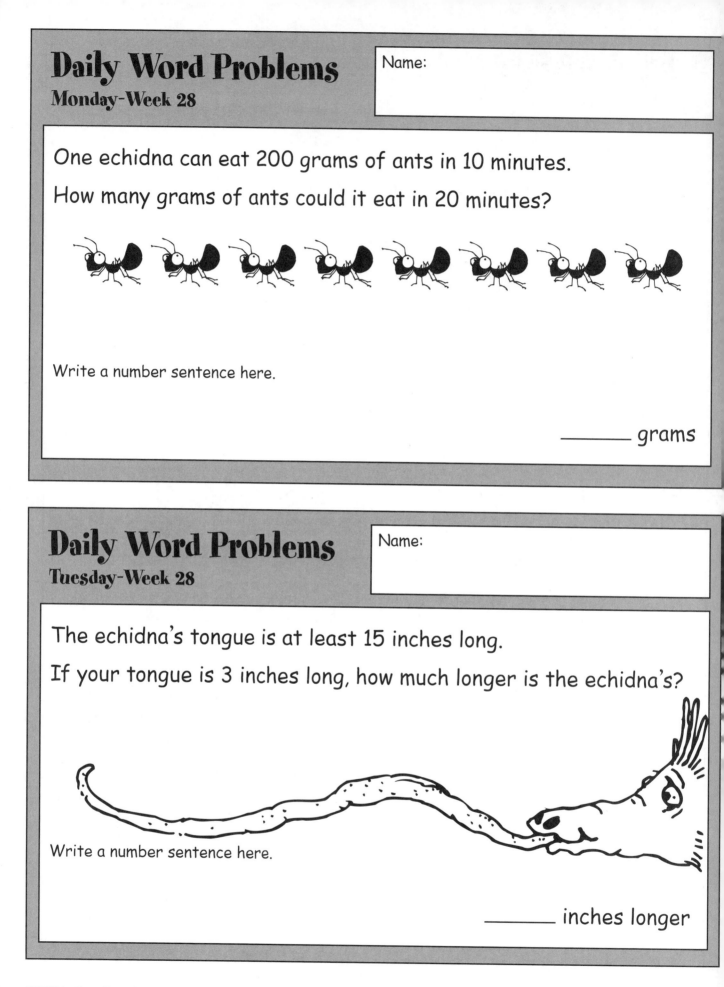

Write a number sentence here.

_____ grams

Daily Word Problems

Tuesday-Week 28

Name:

The echidna's tongue is at least 15 inches long.

If your tongue is 3 inches long, how much longer is the echidna's?

Write a number sentence here.

_____ inches longer

Daily Word Problems

Wednesday-Week 28

Name:

An echidna lays its sticky tongue across an anthill.

Two sets of eight ants climb onto its tongue.

How many ants will the echidna catch?

Write a number sentence here.

_____ ants

Daily Word Problems

Thursday-Week 28

Name:

The echidna's spines are about 5 cm long.

The porcupine's spines are about 13 cm long.

How much longer are the porcupine's spines?

Write a number sentence here.

_____ cm longer

Name:

Echidnas like cool temperatures.

They are active when the temperature is between 60 and 68 degrees Fahrenheit.

Choose the days you might spot an echidna moving about.

○ Monday - 62 degrees

○ Tuesday - 75 degrees

○ Wednesday - 80 degrees

○ Thursday - 69 degrees

○ Friday - 65 degrees

Facts About Echidnas

- Echidnas are good diggers.
- If approached by an enemy, they dig very rapidly straight down.
- In seconds, all that is showing is a small tuft of spines.

Daily Word Problems

Monday-Week 29

Name: _____

The people on the safari saw 7 black rhinos and 9 white rhinos.

How many rhinos did they see in all?

Write a number sentence here.

_____ rhinos

Daily Word Problems

Tuesday-Week 29

Name: _____

The black rhinoceros weighs about 2,000 pounds.

The white rhinoceros weighs about 4,000 pounds.

Which rhinoceros weighs more?

Write a number sentence here.

_____

How much more? _____ pounds

Daily Word Problems

Wednesday–Week 29

Name: _____

There are fewer than 2,550 black rhinos alive today.

Write three numbers that are greater than 2,550.

_____   _____   _____

Write three numbers that are less than 2,550.

_____   _____   _____

Daily Word Problems

Thursday–Week 29

Name: _____

The black rhinoceros is about 11 feet long.

The white rhinoceros is about $12\frac{1}{2}$ feet long.

How much longer is the white rhinoceros?

Write a number sentence here.

_____ feet longer

Name:

White rhinos like to be in a group.

Each group has at least one adult and at least one young rhino.

Tell how many different combinations of adults and young rhinos there could be in a group of seven rhinos.

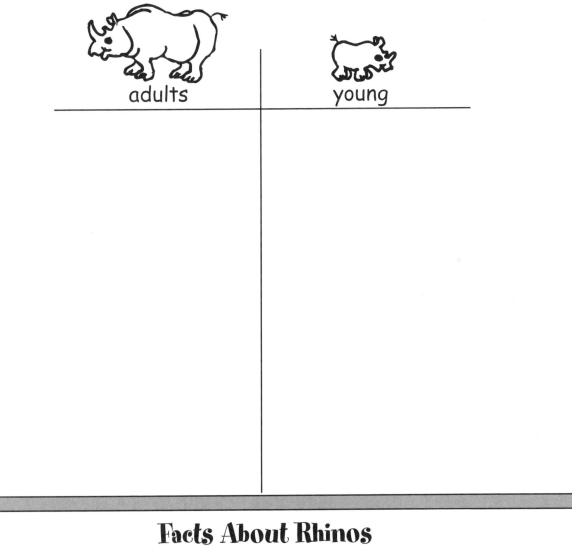

adults | young

Facts About Rhinos

- Rhinos are some of the largest grazing animals alive.
- The black rhino has a pointed, flexible upper lip.
- The lip helps it grab mouthfuls of leaves, buds, and shoots.
- The white rhino has a wide, squared-off lip.
- It eats a wide swath of grass.

Daily Word Problems

Monday-Week 30

Name:

When an alligator's teeth wear out, it grows new ones.

An alligator has about 80 teeth in its mouth at one time.

How many tens are in 80?

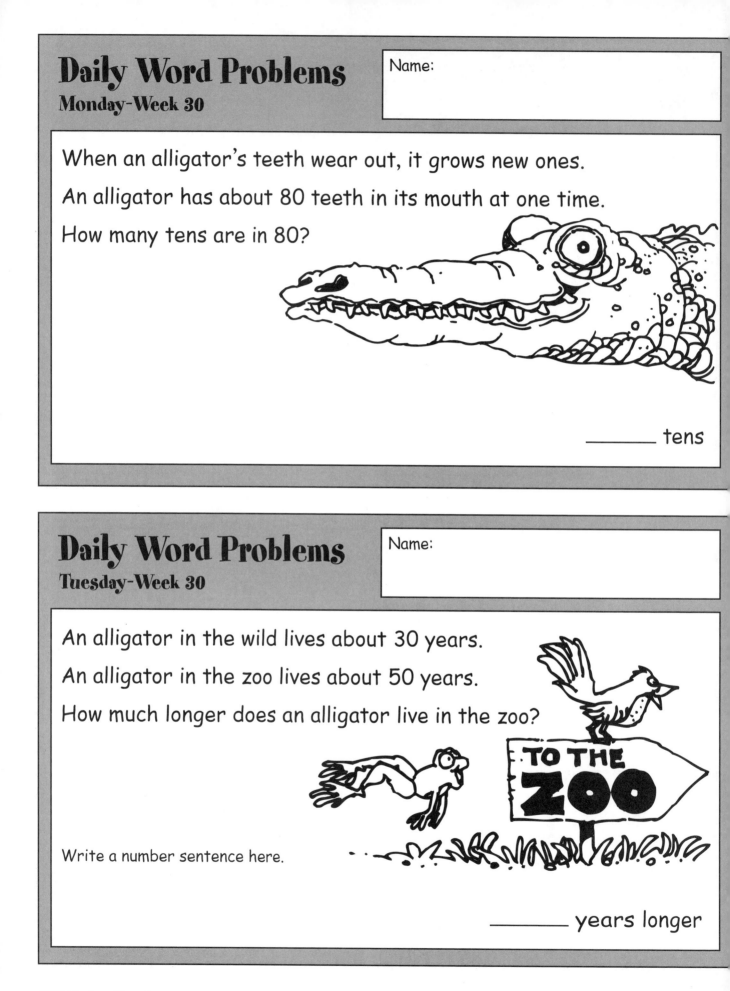

_____ tens

Daily Word Problems

Tuesday-Week 30

Name:

An alligator in the wild lives about 30 years.

An alligator in the zoo lives about 50 years.

How much longer does an alligator live in the zoo?

Write a number sentence here.

_____ years longer

Daily Word Problems

Wednesday-Week 30

Name: _____

An adult male alligator weighs about 500 pounds.

A black rhinoceros weighs 2,000 pounds.

A white rhinoceros weighs 4,000 pounds.

How many alligators weigh as much as a black rhinoceros? _____

How many alligators weigh as much as a white rhinoceros? _____

Daily Word Problems

Thursday-Week 30

Name: _____

Six alligators were resting at the edge of the swamp.

Five more alligators slid into place.

How many alligators were there in all?

If three of the alligators take a swim, how many will be left?

Write number sentences here.

_____ alligators in all

_____ alligators left

Daily Word Problems

Name:

The adult American alligator is a solid dark color. The young alligators are black with bright yellow blotches and stripes.

Finish the pattern in the first column and then make up three different patterns in the other columns. Use **A** to stand for the Adult alligator. Use **Y** to stand for the Young alligator.

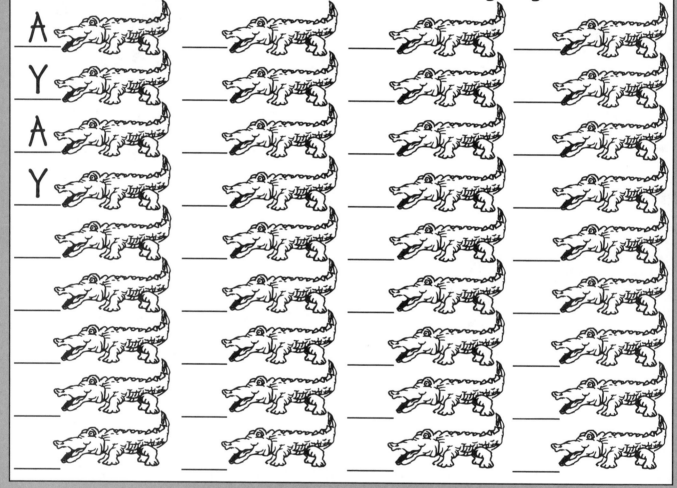

Facts About Alligators

- Alligators make "gator holes" with their large, heavy tails.
- The holes retain water during periods of little rain.
- Gator holes provide water and food for wading birds.
- In turn, the alligators may eat the birds that come to the hole.

Daily Word Problems

Monday-Week 31

Name:

A meerkat uses its tail to balance when it stands upright.

The meerkat is about 12 inches tall and its tail is 8 inches long.

Compare the meerkat's height with its tail length.

Which is more?

○ height   ○ tail length

How much more? _____ inches

Daily Word Problems

Tuesday-Week 31

Name:

The meerkats ate
- three scorpions,
- six beetles,
- seven crickets,
- four eggs, and
- twelve roots.

How many things did they eat in all?

Write a number sentence here.

_____ things

Daily Word Problems

Wednesday-Week 31

Name:

A meerkat mother has five babies each year.

How many babies would she have in seven years?

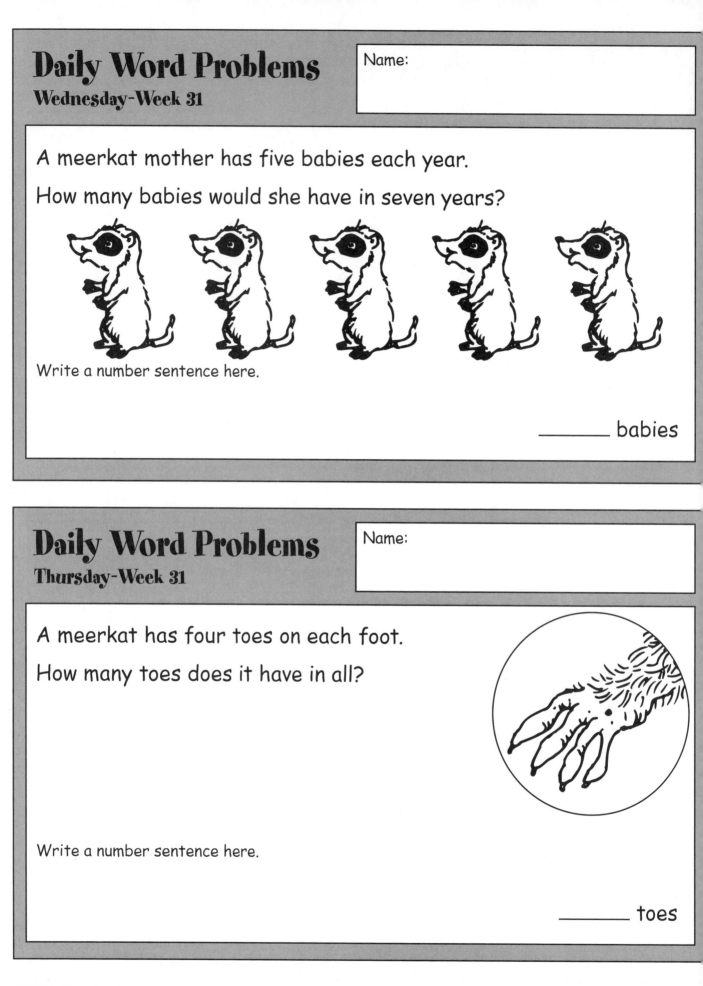

Write a number sentence here.

_____ babies

Daily Word Problems

Thursday-Week 31

Name:

A meerkat has four toes on each foot.

How many toes does it have in all?

Write a number sentence here.

_____ toes

Name:

Meerkats live in groups called mobs or gangs.

The naturalist counted the meerkats in 5 mobs.

How many meerkats are there in all?

Mob 1—10

Mob 2—30

Mob 3—50

Mob 4—5

Mob 5—40

_____ meerkats

Facts About Meerkats

- Meerkats have very good eyesight and hearing.
- They often sit up on their hind legs to look for their next meal.
- They also watch for any sign of danger.

Daily Word Problems

Monday-Week 32

Name:

Baby hedgehogs' spines are under their skin when they are born.

Spines start to appear about 24 hours after birth.

A baby hedgehog is born on Tuesday at 8 p.m.

At what time will its spines appear?

_____

Daily Word Problems

Tuesday-Week 32

Name:

A hedgehog loses $\frac{1}{3}$ of its body weight when it hibernates.

It weighed 600 g when it began hibernating.

How much will it weigh after hibernating?

| 100 g | 100 g | 100 g | 100 g | 100 g | 100 g |

Write a number sentence here.

_____ g

Daily Word Problems

Name:

Newborn hedgehogs weigh about 10 g.

An adult hedgehog weighs 500 g.

How much weight does a hedgehog gain after it is born?

Write a number sentence here.

_____ g

Daily Word Problems

Name:

The pet store sells hedgehog food in a 5-pound bag for $10.00.

A 5-pound bag should last 2 months.

How much will it cost to feed a hedgehog for 10 months?

Write a number sentence here.

$_____

Daily Word Problems

Friday-Week 32

Name: _____

Look at the graph comparing animal heights in inches.
Answer the questions. Give the height of each animal.

Animal Heights

Height (inches)	hedgehog	meerkat	Pacific gecko	sloth	horned frog
25					
24				24	
23					
22					
21					
20					
19					
18					
17					
16					
15					
14					
13					
12		12			
11					
10	10				
9					
8					
7					7
6					
5			5		
4					
3					
2					
1					
0					

Which animal is the tallest? _____

The shortest? _____

Facts About Hedgehogs

- The hedgehog has small eyes and a pointed nose.
- It has spines on its back and a soft underside.
- When it is threatened, it rolls itself into a ball.
- In this position, its spines project in all directions.

Daily Word Problems

Monday-Week 33

Name:

Iguanas have five free toes ending in sharp claws on each foot.

How many claws does an iguana have?

Write a number sentence here.

_____ claws

Daily Word Problems

Tuesday-Week 33

Name:

An iguana mother lays about 50 eggs in a burrow and leaves them.

When the iguana babies hatch, they grow up without her care.

Only 10 babies will survive to become adults.

How many will **not** survive?

Write a number sentence here.

_____ iguanas

Daily Word Problems

Name:

The adult iguana is about 6 feet long.

The young iguana is 12 inches long.

How much will it grow before it is an adult?

Write a number sentence here.

_____ feet

Daily Word Problems

Name:

Iguana eggs hatch in 10 weeks.

How many days is that?

MONDAY   TUESDAY   WEDNESDAY   THURSDAY   FRIDAY   SATURDAY   SUNDAY

Write a number sentence here.

_____ days

The iguana's tail makes up $\frac{1}{2}$ of its length.

If the iguana is 6 feet long, how long is its tail? _____ feet

Facts About Iguanas

- The iguana is a tree-living lizard, but it also swims well.
- It has sharp teeth and claws.
- It defends itself fiercely when attacked.
- It feeds mainly on plants.

Daily Word Problems

Monday-Week 34

Name:

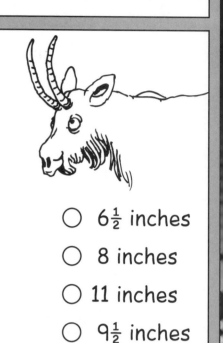

Mountain goats have horns between
6 and 10 inches long.

Which of these lengths fit in this range?

○ 6½ inches

○ 8 inches

○ 11 inches

○ 9½ inches

Daily Word Problems

Tuesday-Week 34

Name:

The mountain goat band had three mothers and four kids.

Another band had three mothers and three kids.

How many goats were in both bands together?

Write a number sentence here.

_____ goats

Daily Word Problems

Wednesday-Week 34

Name: _____

The adult mountain goat is about 40 inches tall at the shoulders.

A yard is 36 inches.

Give the mountain goat's height in yards and inches.

_____ yard, _____ inches

Daily Word Problems

Thursday-Week 34

Name: _____

The mountain goat weighs 250 pounds.

The bobcat weighs 25 pounds.

How much heavier is the mountain goat?

Hint: Think about how many quarters (25 cents) make 50 cents.

Write a number sentence here.

_____ pounds heavier

Name:

The mountain goat can leap 11 feet in a single jump.

Which mountain can it climb?   ○ A   ○ B   ○ C

How many feet does the goat leap to
make it to the top?

_____ feet

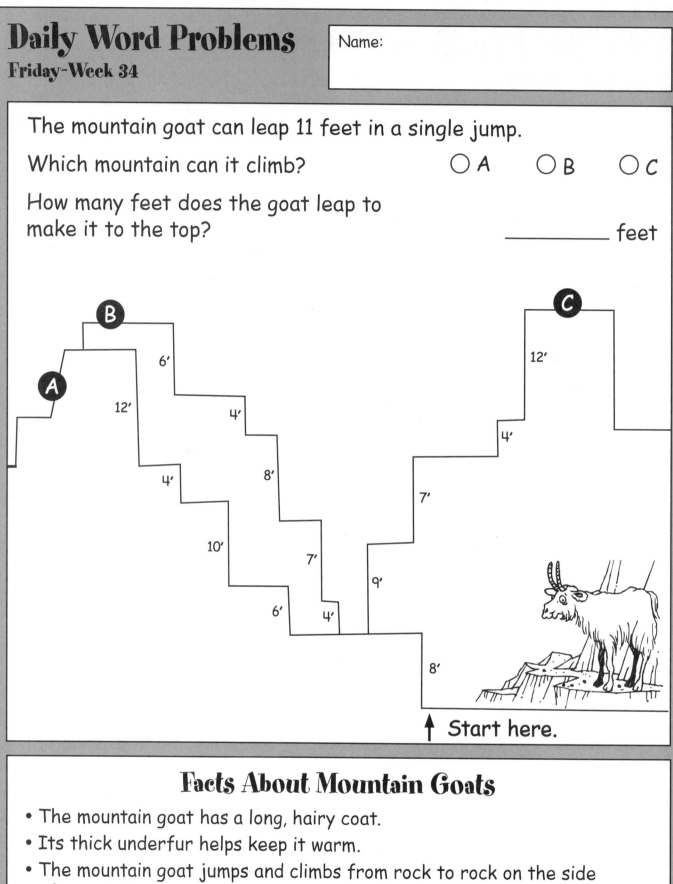

↑ Start here.

Facts About Mountain Goats

- The mountain goat has a long, hairy coat.
- Its thick underfur helps keep it warm.
- The mountain goat jumps and climbs from rock to rock on the side of mountains.

Daily Word Problems

Monday-Week 35

Name: _____

An adult hippopotamus has tusk-like canine teeth.

Each tooth is about 28 inches long.

One human tooth is 2 inches long.

How much longer is the hippo tooth than the human tooth?

Write a number sentence here.

_____ inches longer

Daily Word Problems

Tuesday-Week 35

Name: _____

The hippo can remain under water as long as 25 minutes.

The hippo went under water at 10:00.

At what time would it come up if it stayed under for

5 minutes? _____

10 minutes? _____

20 minutes? _____

25 minutes? _____

Daily Word Problems

Wednesday-Week 35

Name:

The hippo spends most of the day in the water.

Only its eyes, ears, and nostrils stay above the surface.

It may swim 30 km a day in search of food.

How far could the hippo swim in three days?

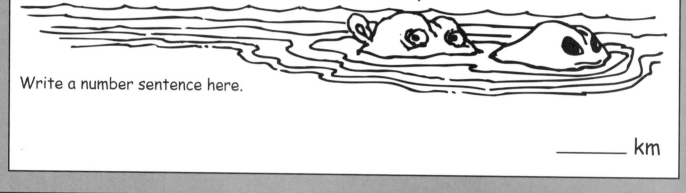

Write a number sentence here.

_____ km

Daily Word Problems

Thursday-Week 35

Name:

One hippo canine tooth weighs 6 pounds.

A hippo has four canine teeth.

How much do the four teeth weigh?

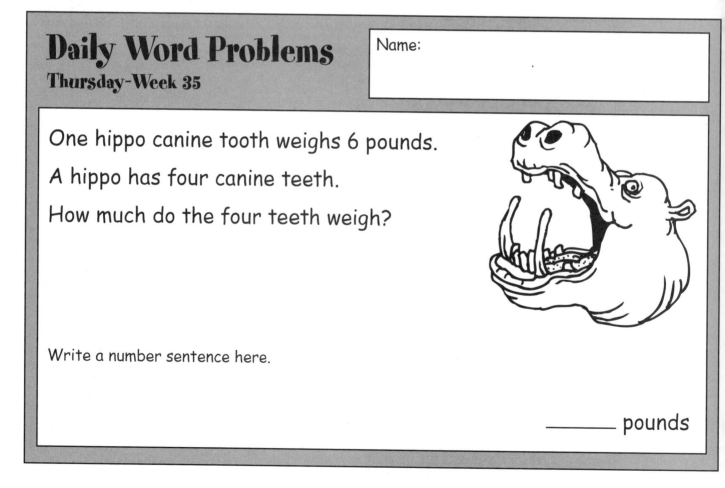

Write a number sentence here.

_____ pounds

Name:

A herd of common hippos is usually made up of 15 animals, including calves, cows, and bulls.

Write six combinations of three numbers that equal 15. The first one has been done for you.

HERD 1 $4 + 9 + 2 = 15$

HERD 2 _____

HERD 3 _____

HERD 4 _____

HERD 5 _____

HERD 6 _____

Facts About Hippos

- The huge hippo swims and dives well.
- It has strong legs and webbed toes.
- It feeds on riverside plants.

Daily Word Problems

Monday-Week 36

Name:

A family group of ostrich hens lay their eggs in one nest.

The ostrich nest has 15 eggs in it.

If 4 eggs hatch, how many eggs will be left?

Write a number sentence here.

_____ eggs

Daily Word Problems

Tuesday-Week 36

Name:

An ostrich cannot fly.

It races across the grass on two legs.

It can go as fast as 44 miles per hour.

The school speed limit for cars is 20 miles per hour.

How much faster can the ostrich go than the cars?

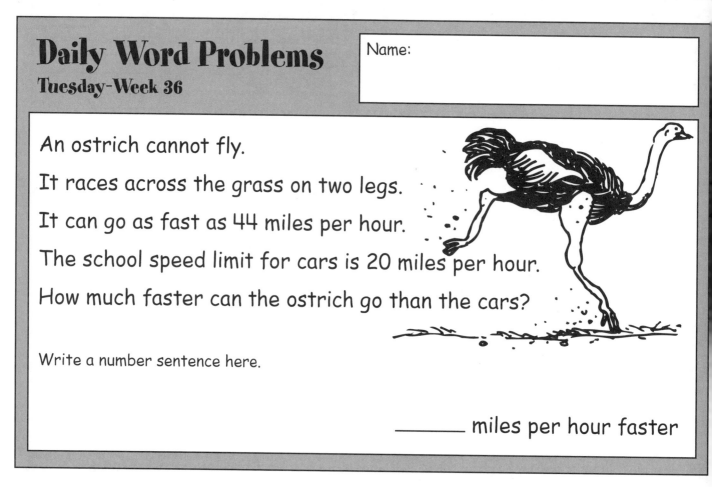

Write a number sentence here.

_____ miles per hour faster

Daily Word Problems
Wednesday-Week 36

Name:

Three mother ostriches and five chicks went for a walk.

How many legs do the ostriches have in all?

Write a number sentence here.

_____ legs

Daily Word Problems
Thursday-Week 36

Name:

One ostrich egg weighs three pounds.

Five kiwi eggs weigh five pounds.

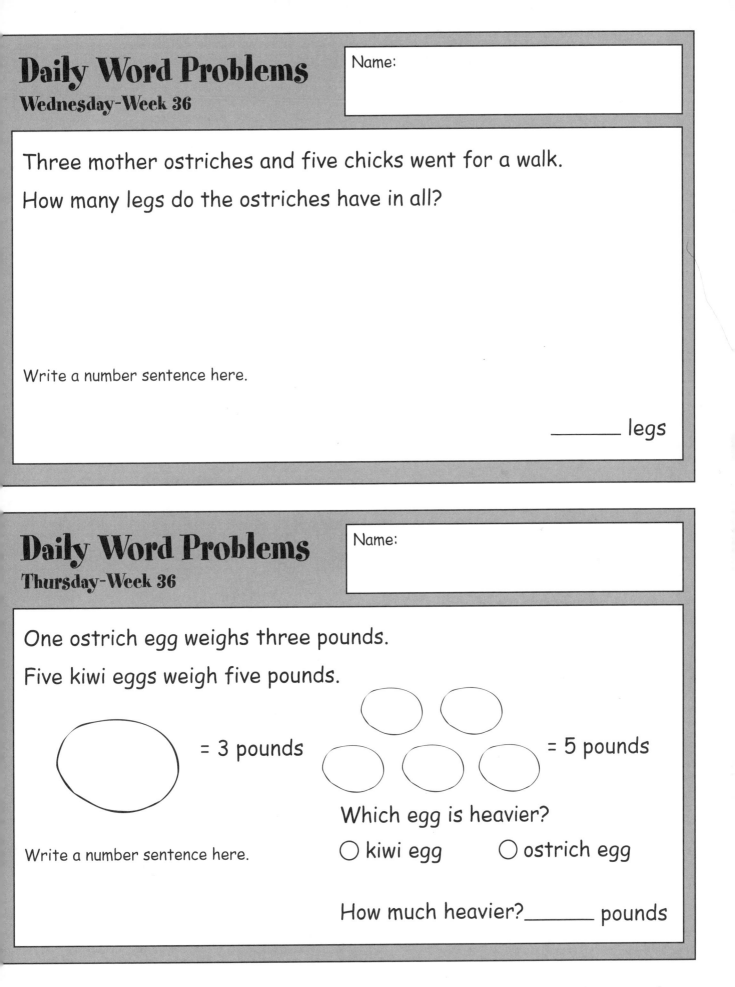

= 3 pounds

= 5 pounds

Write a number sentence here.

Which egg is heavier?

○ kiwi egg   ○ ostrich egg

How much heavier?_____ pounds

Daily Word Problems

Name: _____

The naturalist counted the ostriches on the reserve. Here is her tally sheet:

Males	||||| ||||| |||||	Total = _____
Females	||||| ||||| ||||| ||||| ||||| ||||| |||||	Total = _____
Chicks	||||| ||||| ||||| ||||| ||||| ||||| ||||| ||||| ||||| ||||| ||||| ||||| ||||| |||||	Total = _____

Total the tally marks in each group.

How many ostriches are there in all?

_____ ostriches

Facts About Ostriches

- An ostrich chick has strong legs for running from danger.
- When the chick gets tired of running, it crouches on the ground.
- Its prickly looking feathers help it hide beside the plants.

Answer Key

Week 1
Monday—3 seals
Tuesday—4 fish
Wednesday—a baby seal
Thursday—8 seals
Friday—5 adults, 3 pups, more adults

Week 2
Monday—3 dolphins
Tuesday—bottlenose dolphin
Wednesday—9 fish
Thursday—4 dolphins
Friday—bottlenose dolphin, river dolphin,
       2 feet longer

Week 3
Monday—2 girl babies
Tuesday—40 ears of corn
Wednesday—8 light rings, 15 rings
Thursday—5 raccoons
Friday—15 fish, Monday

Week 4
Monday—yes, $3.00
Tuesday—6 guinea pigs
Wednesday—15 times
Thursday—4 feet, 6 whiskers, 2 ears, 2 eyes, 1 nose
Friday—standing, crouching, standing, crouching;
       black nose, black nose, white nose, black
       nose, black nose, white nose; stripe, no
       stripe, stripe, no stripe; eye closed, eye
       opened, eye closed, eye opened

Week 5
Monday—8 zebras
Tuesday—male
Wednesday—50 miles
Thursday—12 zebras
Friday—middle zebra

Week 6
Monday—1 kitten
Tuesday—7 cans of food
Wednesday—5 kittens
Thursday—18 claws, 36 claws
Friday—16 kittens, Week 4

Week 7
Monday—8 pieces
Tuesday—14 mice
Wednesday—7 mice
Thursday—8 ears, 4 tails, 16 legs
Friday—50 babies, 100 babies

Week 8
Monday—10 nuts
Tuesday—8 quarters
Wednesday—6 squirrels
Thursday—6 times
Friday—5 inches, 4 inches, 6 inches

Week 9
Monday—9 piglets
Tuesday—40 inches longer
Wednesday—500 pounds less
Thursday—12 tusks
Friday—23 warthogs

Week 10
Monday—400 pounds
Tuesday—4 llamas
Wednesday—16 bags of corn
Thursday—10 llamas
Friday—15 bales of hay

Week 11
Monday—10 years longer
Tuesday—17 together
Wednesday—8 termites
Thursday—300 pounds
Friday—6 feet

Week 12
Monday—6 polar bears
Tuesday—male, 330 pounds
Wednesday—40 claws
Thursday—the width of the paw, the width of the paw,
       the length of 3 tails
Friday—10 more teeth

Week 13
Monday—12 feet longer
Tuesday—80 eggs
Wednesday—10 alligators
Thursday—4 feet, 10 feet
Friday—10 trips

Week 14
Monday—4 koalas, 2 koalas, 6 koalas
Tuesday—12 years longer
Wednesday—10 hours
Thursday—50 leaves
Friday—females, 1 more; males, 1 more; 12 koalas

Week 15
Monday—9 feet
Tuesday—7,000 pounds more
Wednesday—17 elephants, 14 elephants
Thursday—yes, yes
Friday—Elephants 1, 2, and 4 should be circled.

Week 16
Monday—7 1/2, 7, 6 1/2, 6, 5 1/2
Tuesday—3 gallons
Wednesday—November, January
Thursday—14 humps
Friday—5 leaves, 6 leaves, 3 leaves, 8 leaves

Week 17
Monday—4 foxes
Tuesday—24 inches
Wednesday—14 mice
Thursday—6 pounds
Friday—From left, clockwise: Fran, Frank, Felix, Flo

Week 18
Monday—40 minutes
Tuesday—7 gallons, 14 gallons, 21 gallons
Wednesday—13 cows
Thursday—20 calves, 40 cattle
Friday—32 teeth

Week 19
Monday—16 toes
Tuesday—10 toes
Wednesday—30 hours, 45 hours
Thursday—12 insects
Friday—alligator, elephant, cow, sloth, mouse

Week 20
Monday—19 walruses
Tuesday—7 clams
Wednesday—100 whiskers
Thursday—yes, yes, yes, Answers will vary.
Friday—

Adults	Babies
0	10
1	9
2	8
3	7
4	6
5	5
6	4
7	3
8	2
9	1
10	0

Week 21
Monday—20 pounds more
Tuesday—3 miles
Wednesday—11 creatures
Thursday—50 degrees cooler
Friday—10 pounds

Week 22
Monday—common porcupine, 6 inches
Tuesday—8 gnawing teeth
Wednesday—14 leaves
Thursday—10 kg more
Friday—29,000 quills

Week 23
Monday—4 times
Tuesday—in a zoo, 3 years
Wednesday—6 feet
Thursday—Sumatran, Siberian, Bengal—
             2 feet longer, 3 feet longer
Friday—Bengal, South Chinese

Week 24
Monday—24,000 tadpoles, 24,000 frogs
Tuesday—24 feet
Wednesday—29 cm longer
Thursday—4 frogs
Friday—3 lizards, 3 mice, 12 bugs, 18 in all

Week 25
Monday—16 days
Tuesday—10 pieces of fruit
Wednesday—male, 200 pounds
Thursday—45 insects
Friday—3 1/2 hours eating, 3 1/2 hours traveling,
             5 hours resting

Week 26
Monday—7 inches
Tuesday—28 feet
Wednesday—14 geckos
Thursday—$10.00
Friday—living room, kitchen, bedroom & family room

Week 27
Monday—4 feet taller
Tuesday—18 feet
Wednesday—1,000 pounds more
Thursday—80 giraffes
Friday—third giraffe

Week 28
Monday—400 grams
Tuesday—12 inches longer
Wednesday—16 ants
Thursday—8 cm longer
Friday—Monday, Friday

Week 29
Monday—16 rhinos
Tuesday—white rhinoceros, 2,000 pounds
Wednesday—Answers will vary.
Thursday—1 1/2 feet longer
Friday—

Adults	Young
1	6
2	5
3	4
4	3
5	2
6	1

Week 30
Monday—8 tens
Tuesday—20 years longer
Wednesday—4 alligators, 8 alligators
Thursday—11 alligators in all, 8 alligators left
Friday—Patterns will vary.

Week 31
Monday—height, 4 inches
Tuesday—32 things
Wednesday—35 babies
Thursday—16 toes
Friday—135 meerkats

Week 32
Monday—Wednesday at 8 p.m.
Tuesday—400 g
Wednesday—490 g
Thursday—$50.00
Friday—sloth—24 inches, Pacific gecko—5 inches